HENRI III AND HIS COURT

BORGO PRESS BOOKS BY ALEXANDRE DUMAS

Anthony
The Barricade at Clichy; or, The Fall of Napoleon
Bathilda
Caligula
The Corsican Brothers
(with Eugène Grangé & Xavier de Montépin)
The Count of Monte Cristo, Part One: The Betrayal of Edmond Dantès
The Count of Monte Cristo, Part Two: The Resurrection of Edmond Dantès
The Count of Monte Cristo, Part Three: The Rise of Monte Cristo
The Count of Monte Cristo, Part Four: The Revenge of Monte Cristo
A Fairy Tale (with Adolphe de Leuven & Léon Lhérie)
The Gold Thieves (with Countess Céleste de Chabrillan)
Henri III and His Court
Kean
The Last of the Three Musketeers (Musketeers #3)
Lorenzino
The Mad Marquis (with Emmanuel Théaulon & Ernest Jaime)
The Mohicans of Paris
Napoléon Bonaparte
Queen Margot
Richard Darlington (with Prosper Dinaux)
Sylvandire
The Three Musketeers (Musketeers #1)
The Three Musketeers—Twenty Years Later
(Musketeers #2)
The Tower of Death (with Frédéric Gaillardet)
The Two Dianas (with Paul Meurice)
Urbain Grandier and the Devils of Loudon
The Venetian
The Whites and the Blues
The Widow's Husband; and, Porthos in Search of an Outfit
Young Louix XIV

RELATED DRAMAS:

The Queen's Necklace, by Pierre Decourcelle
The Seed of the Musketeers, by Paul de Kock & Guénée (Musketeers #5)
The San Felice, by Maurice Drack
The Son of Porthos the Musketeer, by Émile Blavet (Musketeers #4)
A Summer Night's Dream, Adolphe de Leuven & Joseph-Bernard Rosier
*The Widow's Husband; and, Porthos in Search of an Out-
fit: Two Dumasian Comedies*, edited by Frank J. Morlock

HENRI III AND HIS COURT

A PLAY IN FIVE ACTS

ALEXANDRE DUMAS

Adapted and Translated by Frank J. Morlock

THE BORGO PRESS

To the memory of
Michael Burgess
(Robert Reginald)
my editor and friend.

CAST OF CHARACTERS

Henry III, *King of France*

Catherine de Medici, *Queen Mother*

Henry of Lorraine, *Duke of Guise*

Catherine de Cleves, *Duchess of Guise*

Paul Estueret, *Count de Saint-Megrin*

Nogaret de la Valette, *Baron d'Epernon*

Anne d'Arques, *Vicomte de Joyeuse Saint Luc*

Bussy d'Amboise, *favorite of the Duke of Anjou*

Balzac d'Entragues, *called Antraguet*

Come Ruggière, *astrologer*

Saint Paul, *aide de Camp of the Duke of Guise*

Arthur, *page of Duchess of Guise*

Brigard, *shopkeeper*

Bussy Le Clerc, *a procurer*

La Chappelle Marteau, *master of accounts*

Thomas Cruce

Du Halde

Georges, *servant of Saint Megrin*

Madame de Cosse

Marie

A page of Antraguet

ACT I

SCENE 1

A large workroom in the home of Come Ruggière, some instruments of physics and chemistry. A half open window in the rear of the apartment with a telescope.

RUGGIÈRE

(leaning on his elbow, a book of astrology open before him—he measures with a compass. A lamp on a table at the right lights the stage)

Yes—this conjunction seems more powerful and more certain.

(looking at an hour glass)

Soon, nine o'clock. Let me wait till midnight before making the test; will I finally succeed? Will I be able to evoke one of those genies that man, they say, can force to obey despite the fact they are more powerful than he? But if the chain of created beings were to break the man?

(Catherine de Medici enters through a secret door—she wears a black half mask, as Ruggière opens another volume and seems to compare them, and shouts.)

RUGGIÈRE

Uncertainty everywhere.

CATHERINE

Father.

(touching him)

Father.

RUGGIÈRE

Who? Ah, Your Majesty, what—you hazard yourself so late—at nine o'clock in the evening—the Rue de Grenelle—so dangerous and deserted!

CATHERINE

I'm not coming from the Louvre, father, I am coming from the Hotel Soissons which communicates with your retreat by this secret passage.

RUGGIÈRE

I was far from expecting the honor.

CATHERINE

Pardon, Ruggière, if I am interrupting you. In any other circumstance, I would ask your permission to take part in it—but tonight?

RUGGIÈRE

Some misfortune?

CATHERINE

No—no misfortunes are still in the future. You yourself cast the horoscope for the month of July and the result of your calculations was that no real misfortune threatened our person or that of our august son—during its duration—today we are at the 20th and nothing has contradicted your predictions with God's help, it will be completely fulfilled.

RUGGIÈRE

It is a new horoscope that you want, daughter? If you want to come up to the tower with me, your knowledge of astronomy is great enough that you can follow my operations and understand them. The constellations are brilliant.

CATHERINE

No, Ruggière, it's on the earth my eyes are fixed now. Around the sun of royalty circle stars as brilliant and fatal—these are the ones that with your aid, father, I count on being able to conjure with.

RUGGIÈRE

Command, daughter. I am ready to obey you.

CATHERINE

Yes—you are completely devoted to me. But also my protection, while unknown by all, is not useless to you— your reputation makes you plenty of enemies, father.

RUGGIÈRE

I know it.

CATHERINE

La Mole, as he died, swore that the wax figures resembling the King found on the altar and pierced by a dagger to the heart, had been supplied by you—and perhaps the same judges who condemned him would find under the hot ashes of his stake enough fire to light that of Cosimo Ruggière.

RUGGIÈRE

(with fear)

I know it—I know it.

CATHERINE

Don't forget it—remain faithful—and so long as heaven leaves Catherine de Medici life and power— fear nothing. Help me to protect both.

RUGGIÈRE

What can I do for Your Majesty?

CATHERINE

First of all, father, have you joined the League as I told you to do?

RUGGIÈRE

Yes, daughter, the first meeting of the League is to take place right here—for not one of them suspects the high protection with which I am honored by Your Majesty. You see, I have understood you and that I have been about your orders.

CATHERINE

And you've also understood that the echo of their words must be contained in my chambers and not that of the King?

RUGGIÈRE

Yes. Yes.

CATHERINE

And now, father, listen, your profound retreat, your scientific work, allows you little time to follow the intrigues of the Court. And besides, your eyes, accustomed to read in the pure heavens will see poorly in the thick and deceitful atmosphere that surrounds the Court.

RUGGIÈRE

Pardon, daughter—the rumors of the world sometimes even reach here—I know that the King of Navarre and the Duke of Anjou have fled the Court—and retired, one into his Kingdom, the other into his government.

CATHERINE

Let them stay there—they disturb me less in the provinces than in Paris—the frank character of the King of Navarre, the irresolute character of the Duke do not threaten us with great dangers—Our enemies are closer to us. You heard tell of the bloody duel that took place on the 27th of April near the Port Saint Antoine between six young men of the Court; four among them were killed, three were favorites of the King.

RUGGIÈRE

I know of his sorrow. I saw the magnificent tombs he raised to Quelus, Schomberg and Mangiron—it showed his great friendship to them. But what could earthly science do against the nineteen sword blows they received? Antraguet, his murderer, ought at least to have been punished by exile.

CATHERINE

Yes, father—but that sadness waned much more quickly as it was exaggerated. Quelus, Schomberg and Mangiron have been replaced by D'Epernon, Joyeuse and Saint Megrin—Antraguet will reappear at Court tomorrow. The Duke of Guise, demands it, and Henry can refuse nothing to his cousin Guise. Saint Megrin and he are my enemies—this young gentleman from Bordeaux worries me. More informed, less frivolous, especially than Joyeuse and D'Epernon, he's acquired an ascendancy over Henry which terrifies me—father, he can make a King out of him.

RUGGIÈRE

And the Duke of Guise?

CATHERINE

He will make a monk out of him—I don't want either. It was necessary for me to make him a bit more than an infant and a little less than a man. Have I filled his heart with vices, weakened his reason with superstitious practices for anyone other than myself to control his wit and divert his taste? No, I've given him an artificial character so that his character would belong to me. All the calculations of my politics, all the resources of my imagination are directed there. It was necessary to remain Regent of France, even though France had a King—it's necessary that one day it will be possible to say "Henry III reigned under Catherine de Medici." I have succeeded up till now— but these two men—

RUGGIÈRE

Well, Rene, your valet de chamber can prepare for them some perfumed gloves such as those you sent Jeanne D'Albrecht—two days before her death, can't he?

CATHERINE

No, they are necessary to me. They keep the King irresolute, which creates my strength. What I need is for some other passions to be cast in the way of their political projects, to distract them for a moment, then I pass between them, reach the King, whom I've isolated with his weakness and seize my power back— I've found a way. The young Saint Megrin is amorous of the Duchess de Guise.

RUGGIÈRE

And as for her?

CATHERINE

Loves him, too, but without confessing it even to herself, perhaps—she is a slave to her reputation for virtue. They are at the point where all they need is an opportunity, a meeting, a tête-à-tête, for the intrigue to develop fully. She herself fears her weakness for she flees him. Father, they will see each other today—they will see each other alone.

RUGGIÈRE

Where will they see each other?

CATHERINE

Here—yesterday, in the club, I heard Joyeuse and D'Epernon, agree together with Saint Megrin to come here—Draw from him a confession of his love, exalt his passion—tell him he is loved. That, thanks to your tact, you can serve him—offer him a tête-à-tête—

(pointing to an alcove hidden in the woodwork)

The Duchess de Guise is already there, in that cabinet so well hidden in the woodwork, that you made so I can hear and see, at need without being seen— By our Lady! It has already been useful to us, to you for your magic operations.

RUGGIÈRE

And how did you get her to come?

CATHERINE

(opening the secret door)

Do you think I consulted her will?

RUGGIÈRE

Then you made her enter through the door which gives on the secret passage?

CATHERINE

Doubtless.

RUGGIÈRE

And have you thought about the perils you are exposing your goddaughter to? The love of Saint Megrin, the jealousy of the Duke, her husband.

CATHERINE

It's exactly that love and that jealousy I have need of. The Duke will go too far if we don't stop him. We will give him something to keep him busy. Anyway, you know the maxim. One must do and attempt whatever to defeat one's enemy—

RUGGIÈRE

So, daughter, you've consented to reveal to her the secret of this alcove?

CATHERINE

She's sleeping. I invited her to take a cup of that liquor that you extract from Arab beans and which you brought from your voyages—and I mixed in some drops of narcotic that I asked of you for this sort of thing.

RUGGIÈRE

Her sleep must be very deep for the virtue of this liquor is sovereign.

CATHERINE

Yes—and can you extract her from this sleep at your will?

RUGGIÈRE

Immediately, if you want it?

CATHERINE

Be careful.

RUGGIÈRE

I think I also told you that on her awakening her ideas will be confused for some time and that her memory will only return as objects strike her eyes.

CATHERINE

Yes—so much the better! She will be less able to account for your magic—as for Saint Megrin, he is like all young men—superstitious and credulous—he loves; he will believe—anyway you won't give her time to recognize anything, you must have a way to open this alcove without leaving this room.

RUGGIÈRE

It's only necessary to lean on a spring hidden in the ornaments of this magic mirror.

(leans on spring and the door of the alcove half rises)

CATHERINE

Your cleverness will do the rest, father, and I rely on you. What time to you expect them?

RUGGIÈRE

I cannot tell you. The presence of Your Majesty made me forget to turn the hourglass—I'll have to call someone.

CATHERINE

No need—they shouldn't be late—that's what's important. Only, father, I'll have a clock brought from Italy—a clock for you or rather write yourself to Florence and ask for it, no matter the cost.

RUGGIÈRE

Your Majesty fulfills all my desires. For a long while, I've wanted to buy one, if one could meet the exorbitant price put on it.

CATHERINE

Why not address yourself to me, father? By Our Lady! It would be vain to see me allow a savant like you lack money. No—come tomorrow, be at the Louvre, be at our Hotel de Soissons—and an order to pay by our royal hand drawn on the superintendent of our finances, will prove to you we are neither forgetful nor ungrateful. God be with you, father!

(She replaces her mask and leaves by the secret door.)

RUGGIÈRE

Yes, I will remind you of your promise. It's only with gold that I can obtain these precious manuscripts that are so—necessary to me—

(listening)

Some one's knocking—it's them—

(shutting the alcove door)

D'EPERNON

(at the back of the stage)

Hello—hey!

RUGGIÈRE

Come ahead, gentlemen, come ahead.

D'EPERNON

(to Joyeuse who enters leaning on a long tube and on Saint Megrin)

Come, come, courage, Joyeuse—here's our sorcerer at last! Live God! Father—you need the legs of a stag and the eyes of a screech owl to get to you.

RUGGIÈRE

The eagle builds his eyrie atop the rocks to be able to see further.

JOYEUSE

(stretching in an armchair)

Yes, but they can see clearly to get there at least.

SAINT MEGRIN

Come, come, gentlemen, it's likely that the savant Ruggière wasn't expecting our visit, otherwise we would have found the antechamber better lit.

RUGGIÈRE

You are mistaken, Count de Saint Megrin. I was expecting you.

D'EPERNON

Then you wrote him?

SAINT MEGRIN

No—on my soul. And I've spoken to no one.

D'EPERNON

(to Joyeuse)

And you?

JOYEUSE

Me? You know I only write when I am forced to. It wears me out!

RUGGIÈRE

I was expecting you, gentlemen and I've been concerned about you.

SAINT MEGRIN

In that case, you know who brings us here.

RUGGIÈRE

Yes.

(D'Epernon and Saint Megrin approach him as does Joyeuse but without getting up from his armchair.)

D'EPERNON

Then all your sorcery is ready in advance. We can question you and you will answer?

RUGGIÈRE

Yes.

JOYEUSE

Our moment, by God's Hand.

(pulling Ruggière to him)

Come here, father. They say you are in commerce with Satan. If that's so, if this conversation with you could compromise our good—I hope you'll think twice before damning three gentlemen from the best families in France.

D'EPERNON

Joyeuse is right—and we are very good Christians.

RUGGIÈRE

Reassure yourselves, gentlemen, I am as good a Christian as yourselves.

D'EPERNON

Since you assure us that you're sorcery has nothing in common with hell—look, what do you need, my head or my hand?

RUGGIÈRE

Neither. Such formalities are good for the vulgar, but you, young man, you are placed high enough above the crowd to be a brilliant star, like those in which I read your destiny. Nogaret de la Valette, Baron D'Epernon.

D'EPERNON

What! You know me, as well? Indeed—there's nothing surprising in that. I've become so popular!

RUGGIÈRE

(continuing)

Nogaret de la Valette, Baron D'Epernon, your past glory is nothing compared to what your future glory will be.

D'EPERNON

Long live God—father—and how shall I go further? The King calls me his son.

RUGGIÈRE

That title is given to you from his friendship alone— and the friendship of kings is fickle—he will call you his brother and the bonds of blood will command it of him.

D'EPERNON

What? You know about the projected marriage?

RUGGIÈRE

She is beautiful, the Princess Christine. Happy will be he who possesses her.

D'EPERNON

But who could have told you this?

RUGGIÈRE

Didn't I tell you young man, your star shines brighter than all others? And now to you, Anne D'Arques, Vicomte Joyeuse—whom the King also calls his child.

JOYEUSE

Well, father, since you read the heavens so well, you must see my wish to pass the time in this excellent chair—so long as it doesn't ruin my horoscope. No— well, go on, I am listening to you.

RUGGIÈRE

Young man, have you thought sometimes, in your ambitious dreams that the Vicomte de Joyeuse might be changed into a Duke—that the title of peer would place you above all the peers of France except the Princes of the Blood and the Royal houses of Savoy, Lorraine and Cleves? Yes—well, you haven't foreseen the half of your fortune. Greetings to the spouse of Marguerite de Vaudemont, sister of the Queen. Hail Grand Admiral of the Kingdom of France.

JOYEUSE

(rising excitedly)

With the help of God and my sword, father, we shall get there!

(giving him his purse)

Here, this is small recompense for the prediction of such a great destiny. But, it's all I have on me.

D'EPERNON

By God, you remind me—I was forgetting—

(fumbling in his purse)

Ah—all we have are some pellets for the pea shooter— I appear to have lost all my Spanish coins at cards. I don't know what's become of this cursed money—it must be dead—long live God! Saint Megrin, you, who are a friend of Ronsard, you ought indeed to charge him for his epitaph.

SAINT MEGRIN

It's buried in the pockets of those rogue Leaguers. I don't think you'll find any gold pieces or Spanish doubloons—still, I've got a few left and if you like—

D'EPERNON

(laughing)

No, keep it to buy some hellebore—for you must know, father, our comrade Saint Megrin has been mad for some time. Only his madness isn't gay—now, he's just given me a great idea. It's necessary that I make some of those Leaguers pay you for my horoscope—let's see, what am I going to do to give you a reward? Help me, Duke de Joyeuse—that title sounds nice, doesn't it. Let's see—think.

JOYEUSE

What do you say to our Master of Accounts—La Chapelle Marteau.

D'EPERNON

Insolvent. In a week he will exhaust the treasures of Philip II.

SAINT MEGRIN

And little Brigard?

D'EPERNON

Bah—a supplier to shopkeepers. He'll offer to pay in tobacco or cinnamon.

RUGGIÈRE

Thomas Cruce will.

D'EPERNON

If I took you at your word, father, your shoulders would be angry for some time with your tongue. He isn't meek.

JOYEUSE

Well—Bussy Le Clerc.

D'EPERNON

Long live God! A procurer—you are a good advisor, Joyeuse.

(to Ruggière)

Here—here's an order for ten doubloons. Go to the home of that Rogue of a Leaguer and make him pay you—if he refuses—tell him I will come myself with twenty gentlemen and a dozen pages or so—

SAINT MEGRIN

Let's go—now your bill is paid, I will remind you that they are expecting us at the Louvre—We must go back, gentlemen—let's go.

JOYEUSE

You are right—we won't be able to find chaises to carry us.

RUGGIÈRE

(stopping Saint Megrin)

What! Young man, you are leaving without consulting me?

SAINT MEGRIN

I am not ambitious father. What could you promise me?

RUGGIÈRE

You are not ambitious! Not in love at least!

SAINT MEGRIN

What are you saying, father! Speak low!

RUGGIÈRE

You are not ambitious young man, and to become the lady of your thoughts, a woman must write in her coat of arms the emblems of two royal houses, surmounted with a Ducal Crown.

SAINT MEGRIN

Lower father, lower!

RUGGIÈRE

Well—do you still doubt the science?

SAINT MEGRIN

No.

RUGGIÈRE

Do you still want to leave without consulting me?

SAINT MEGRIN

Perhaps, I ought to.

RUGGIÈRE

I have yet more revelations for you.

SAINT MEGRIN

Whether they come from heaven or from hell, I will hear them. Joyeuse, D'Epernon, leave me—I will rejoin you soon in the antechamber.

JOYEUSE

A moment! A moment! My pea shooter! By Saint Anne! If I see the house of a Leaguer at fifty paces, I don't intend to leave him a single window unbroken.

D'EPERNON

(To Saint Megrin)

Come—hurry up—and we'll give you good protection in the meantime.

(They leave.)

SAINT MEGRIN

(pushing the door)

Right, right.

(returning)

Father, a single word—Does she love me? You are silent, father. Curses! Oh—make her—make her love me. They say your art has unknown resources—brews, love potions—! Whatever your ways are, I accept them, though they ruin my life in this world and my salvation in the next. I am rich. All that I have is yours. Gold, jewels—ah, perhaps your science scorns the treasures of this world. Well, hear me, father, they say that magicians sometimes require for their cabalistic experiments the blood of a still living man—

(presenting his naked arm)

Here, father! Just promise to make me loved by her.

RUGGIÈRE

Why are you certain she doesn't love you?

SAINT MEGRIN

What can I tell you, father? Unto that very hour of despair, in the depth of the heart there remains a weighty hope. Yes, sometimes I thought I could read it in her eyes when she didn't turn away fast enough. But I may be deceiving myself—she flees me and I am unable to find myself alone with her.

RUGGIÈRE

And if you were to finally succeed in that?

SAINT MEGRIN

Father—were that the case, her first word would tell me what I have to fear or to hope.

RUGGIÈRE

Well—come and look in this mirror. They call it the mirror of reflection—is this the person you desire to see there?

SAINT MEGRIN

It's she—father.

> *(as he looks, the alcove opens behind him and the sleeping Duchess de Guise can be seen)*

RUGGIÈRE

Look—

SAINT MEGRIN

God—the true God! It's she! She—sleeping—ah, Catherine.

(the alcove shuts)

Catherine! Nothing.

(looking behind him)

Nothing more this way—everything has vanished. It was a dream—an illusion—father—let me see her—let me see her again.

RUGGIÈRE

She's sleeping, you say?

SAINT MEGRIN

Yes.

RUGGIÈRE

Listen. It is especially during sleep that our power is greatest—I can profit by hers to transport her here.

SAINT MEGRIN

Here, near me?

RUGGIÈRE

But as soon as she wakes up, remember my power can do nothing contrary to her will.

SAINT MEGRIN

Fine—but hurry, father, hurry.

RUGGIÈRE

Take this flask—all you need to do is to make her breathe it for her to come to—

SAINT MEGRIN

Yes, yes, but hurry—

RUGGIÈRE

Do you undertake an oath never to reveal this?

SAINT MEGRIN

By the place I hope for in paradise, I swear it to you.

RUGGIÈRE

Well, read!

(While Saint Megrin runs over some lines in a book given him by Ruggière, the alcove behind him opens, a spring pushes the sofa forward and the alcove closes.)

RUGGIÈRE

Look!

(The alcove closes and Ruggière leaves.)

SAINT MEGRIN

She! It's she! Right there.

(rushing toward her then stopping)

God! I've read that sometimes these magicians raise bodies from the tomb which from the power of their enchantments take on the semblance of a living person. If—may God protect me—ah! Nothing changes—it's not a trick—a dream from heaven. Oh—her heart is hardly beating—her hand—she's icy. Catherine— wake up—this sleep terrifies me—Catherine! She's sleeping—what to do? Ah—this flask—I was forgetting. My head is lost!

(he makes her breathe the flask)

DUCHESS

Ah!

SAINT MEGRIN

Yes—yes—breathe! Get up—speak! Speak! I prefer to hear your voice even if it banishes me forever from your presence than to see you sleep this cold slumber.

DUCHESS

Ah! How weak I am!

(she rises and leans her head on Saint Megrin, who is at her feet)

I slept a long while—my women—how to call them?

(noticing Saint Megrin)

Ah, it's you, count?

(she offers him her hand)

SAINT MEGRIN

Yes—yes.

DUCHESS

You! But why you? It's not you I am accustomed to see when I wake up. My head is so heavy that I cannot gather my thoughts.

SAINT MEGRIN

Oh—Catherine—let one idea alone come to you—let one idea remain—that of my love for you.

DUCHESS

Yes, yes, you love me—oh, I've noticed—for a long while—and me too, I've loved you and I've hidden it from you. Why then? It seems to me there's a great deal of joy to say that.

SAINT MEGRIN

Oh—say it again—say it—for it is a great joy to hear it.

DUCHESS

But I had a reason for hiding it from you. What was it? Ah! It wasn't you I ought to love.

(rising and forgetting her handkerchief on the sofa)

Holy Mother of God, have I said that I love you? Wretch that I am! My love woke up before my reason.

SAINT MEGRIN

Catherine! only listen to your heart! You love me! You love me.

DUCHESS

Me? I didn't say that, Count—it's not so—don't believe it—it was a lie—sleep—the—but how did I get here— what is this room? Marie! Madame de Cosse—leave me, Count—go away.

SAINT MEGRIN

Go away! And why?

DUCHESS

Oh, My God! My God!—what's happening to me?

SAINT MEGRIN

Madame—I see myself here, I found you, I don't know how. It's an enchantment, magic.

DUCHESS

I am ruined! I, who up to now have fled you—I who am already suspected by the Duke, my lord and master.

SAINT MEGRIN

The Duke de Guise, a thousand damnations—the Duke, your lord and master—oh, if he dared to even suspect you wrongly—all his blood—and mine—

DUCHESS

Count—you terrify me.

SAINT MEGRIN

Pardon—but when I think I could know you free—to be loved by you—become also your lord and master— the Duke wrongs me greatly—may my good angel fail me at the day of judgment if I don't pay him for it.

DUCHESS

Count! But yet—where am I?—tell me—help me to leave here—to return to my palace—and I will forgive you.

SAINT MEGRIN

Forgive me—and what then is my offense?

DUCHESS

I am here—and you ask me that! You have profited by her sleep to abduct a woman to whom you are a stranger—who cannot love you—who does not love you—sir—

SAINT MEGRIN

Who doesn't love me! Ah, Madame, no one who loves as I do is not loved in return. I believe your first words. I believe them!

DUCHESS

Silence!

SAINT MEGRIN

Don't be afraid.

JOYEUSE

(in the antechamber)

Live God! We are on watch and no one passes.

THE VOICE OF THE DUKE

By God's Head—gentlemen, take care—in thinking to tease a fox you may awaken a lion.

DUCHESS

Holy Mary! That's the voice of the Duke—where to flee—where to hide?

SAINT MEGRIN

It's the Duke of Guise—well—

(rushing toward the door)

DUCHESS

Stop, sir—in the name of God! You will ruin me.

SAINT MEGRIN

It's true—

(runs and bars the door)

RUGGIÈRE

(entering and taking the Duchess by the hand)

Silence, Madame, follow me!

(he opens the secret door, the Duchess rushes out. Ruggière follows her. The door shuts behind them)

DUKE

(impatiently)

Gentlemen!

D'EPERNON

Don't you think he has a bit of a Lorraine accent which is agreeable?

SAINT MEGRIN

(returning)

Now, Madame—we can—well—where is she? Can all this be the work of the demon? What to think? Oh, my head! My head!

DUKE

(entering)

I should have guessed from those in the antechamber who would do me the honor of the apartment.

SAINT MEGRIN

Don't take it ill, Duke, I don't profit from the chance to render you all those honors of which I believe you are worthy. The time will come, I hope.

JOYEUSE

Ah—Saint Megrin—it's Scarface himself.

SAINT MEGRIN

Yes, yes, gentlemen—it's he—but he'll make us late— let's get going—let's leave.

(They leave.)

DUKE

When will some sharp-shooters deliver us from these insolent little dandies? The Count Caussade de St. Megrin. The King made him Count—and who knows where he'll stop, this little mushroom of fortune? My brother, Mayenne, before his departure, recommended him to me. I ought to be careful, he told me—he thought he noticed that he loved the Duchess and warned me through Bassompiere. God's Head—if I weren't so sure of the virtue of my wife, the Count de Saint Megrin would pay dearly for that suspicion.

(Enter Ruggière.)

DUKE

Ah, it's you Ruggière.

RUGGIÈRE

Yes, Milord, Duke.

DUKE

I've advanced the meeting that is to take place here by one day. In a few minutes, our friends will be here. I came first because I wanted to find you alone. Nicholas Poulain told me I could count on you.

RUGGIÈRE

He speaks the truth—and my art—

DUKE

Let's not discuss your art—whether I believe it or I don't believe it, I am much too good a Christian to have recourse to it. But I know you are wise, versed in the knowledge of manuscripts and archives—that is the science that I need. Listen to me. The lawyer, John David, has been able to obtain the Holy Father's approval of the League. He's back in France.

RUGGIÈRE

Yes, the last letters that I received from him were dated from Lyon.

DUKE

He is dead. He was the bearer of important documents. These documents have been stolen. Among them a genealogy of my family that my father of glorious memory had prepared by Francis Rosieres in 1535. That proved that the princes of Lorraine were the sole and true descendants of Charlemagne. Father, I must have a new family tree that has its roots in the Carolingians—it must be supported by new evidence. This is hard and difficult work which will be well paid. Here's an installment.

RUGGIÈRE

Milord, you will be satisfied with me.

DUKE

Fine—and what did those young court butterflies come here to do?

RUGGIÈRE

To consult me about the future.

DUKE

Are they then unhappy with the present? The future will really be difficult for them. They must be really spoiled! They've gone, haven't they ?

RUGGIÈRE

Yes, Milord, they are at the Louvre now.

DUKE

Let the Valois sleep to the sound of their buzzing so as not to awaken the one for whom the bell will soon toll. But there's someone in the antechamber. Ah, it's Father Cruce.

(Cruce enters.)

DUKE

Ah, it's you —what news?

CRUCE

Bad, Milord, bad—nothing is going right—everything degenerates. By God—we are good weather conspirators.

DUKE

Why's that?

CRUCE

Eh! Yes—we are wasting time in political nonsense we are running from door to door to make enemies join the League. By Saint Thomas—you don't have to show yourself, Duke—when they look at you, the Huguenots want no part of the League.

DUKE

Is this your list?

CRUCE

Three or 400 zealots have signed, 500 enemies of the League have put their initials—some thirty or so of the Huguenots refused with a scowl. As for them, I've put a white cross on their door, and if ever the occasion presents itself of discharging my poor blunderbuss which has been unused for six years—but I won't have that joy, Milord—those good traditions are ruined. By God's Head, if I were in your place—

DUKE

And the list?

CRUCE

Here it is. Use it to make wads for blunderbusses, Duke and sooner, rather than later.

DUKE

That will come, my brave man, that will come.

CRUCE

May God will it! Ah! Ah—here are the comrades.

(Enter Bussy Le Clerc, La Chappelle-Marteau, and

Brigard.)

DUKE

Well, gentlemen, was the harvest good?

BUSSY LE CLERC

Not bad—200 or 300 signatures for my part—some lawyers and procurers.

CRUCE

And you, my little Brigard? Did you make the shopkeepers march?

BRIGARD

They've all signed.

CRUCE

(striking him on the shoulder)

Long live God! Behold a zealot, Duke. All those of the League can present themselves at his shop on the corner of the Rue Aubrey le Boucher—they will have a rebate of thirty cents a pound on all they buy.

DUKE

And you, Marteau?

LA CHAPPELLE-MARTEAU

Less lucky, Milord—the Masters of accounts are afraid—the President to Parliament only signed with reservations.

DUKE

Your President has royal fleur de lys growing apace in his heart. Didn't he see the promise of obedience to the King and his family?

LA CHAPPELLE-MARTEAU

Yes—but it was added without his permission.

DUKE

He's right, Your President. I will appear tomorrow at His Majesty's levy, gentlemen. My first act ought to have been to obtain the sanction of the King. He wouldn't have dared to refuse it to me. But, thank God—it's not yet too late. Tomorrow I shall place before King Henry of Valois, the situation in his realm! I will explain to him the discontents of his subjects. He has already tacitly recognized the League. I want him to publicly name the leader for it.

LA CHAPPELLE-MARTEAU

Take care, Milord—the powder isn't far from the trigger of a pistol, and some new assassin—like the patriot who killed your father—

DUKE

He wouldn't dare—besides I will go armed.

CRUCE

May God be for you and the Good Cause—that done, Milord, I believe it will be time for you to decide.

DUKE

Oh, my decision was taken long ago—what I don't decide in an hour, I don't decide all my life.

CRUCE

Yes, and with your prudence, all your life may perhaps not suffice to execute what you decided in a quarter of an hour.

DUKE

Mr. Cruce—in a project like ours time is the ally of the most cautious.

CRUCE

God's Head! You have to time to wait—but as for me, I am in a hurry and since everyone has signed—

DUKE

Yes—and the 12,000 men—many Swiss and cavalry men—that His Majesty has just brought in to the good city of Paris? Have they signed? Each one carries a blunderbuss, mounted with a pretty

wick, Mr. Cruce—not counting the small cannon of the Bastille—
leave it to me to set the day—and when it comes—

BUSSY LE CLERC

Well—what will we do to the King?

DUKE

What Madame Montpensier promised him yesterday pointing to a
pair of scissors—a monk's crown.

BUSSY LE CLERC

Then so be it! Right, my old sorcerer? For I presume you are of our
opinion since you don't say anything.

RUGGIÈRE

I was waiting for a favorable opportunity to present a small request.

BUSSY LE CLERC

What?

RUGGIÈRE

(giving the letter from D'Epernon)

Here.

BUSSY LE CLERC

What? A bill from D'Epernon—drawn on me—this is a joke.

RUGGIÈRE

He said that if you didn't honor it he would find you and make you
pay it himself.

BUSSY LE CLERC

Let him come—has he forgotten that before being procurer I was
Master of Arms in the Regiment of Lorraine. I think the dear favorite must be jealous of the statues which decorate the tombs of

Quelus and Mangiron? Well—that won't keep us from dressing him in marble in his turn.

DUKE

Be careful, Master Bussy! I wouldn't have such an enemy for twenty-five of my friends—he's enrolling recruits for us. Give me the bill, Ruggière—ten crown—here.

BUSSY LE CLERC

What are you doing, Milord?

DUKE

Don't worry. When the moment comes to settle accounts. I'll arrange matters so he doesn't remain my debtor. But it's getting late. Till tomorrow evening, gentlemen. The doors of the Hotel de Guise will be open to all our friends. Madame de Montpensier will do the honors. And doubly well received by her will be those who come with the double cross of Lorraine. So it's agreed—till tomorrow night at the Hotel de Guise.

CRUCE

Yes, Milord.

(They all leave except the Duke.)

DUKE

(sitting on the sofa where the Duchess dropped her handkerchief)

By Saint Henry of Lorraine! It's a rough job I've undertaken. These folks think one reaches the throne of France like a church benefice in the Provinces. The Duke of Guise—King of France—that's a beautiful dream. It will come—still—but above all there are rivals to combat! The King's younger brother, the Duke of Anjou—first of all—though he's the least to be feared, he's hated equally by the people and the nobility and he will easily enough be declared a heretic and barred from succession—but in his default, King Philip of Spain—is he ready to claim under the title of brother-in-law, the inheritance of the House of Valois? The Duke of Savoy, his uncle by marriage, would raise pretensions. A Duke of Lorraine married his sister. Perhaps there would be a way—that would be to pass the crown of France to the head of an old Bourbon Cardinal and to force him to recognize me as his heir. I'll think about it. How many troubles, torments—only to end perhaps by the ball of a pistol or the blade of a dagger— Ah—

(he drops his hand in discouragement—it rests on the handkerchief forgotten by the Duchess)

What's this?—This kerchief belongs to the Duchess of Guise— here are the arms of Cleves and Lorraine joined together. She came here! Saint Megrin! Oh, Mayenne! Mayenne! So you were not wrong—and he—he—

(calling)

Saint Paul!

(his squire enters)

I am going—Saint Paul, search out for me the same men who murdered Dugast.

CURTAIN

ACT II

SCENE 2

A hall in the Louvre.

To the left, two armchairs and some stools prepared for the King, the Queen Mother and the some courtiers. Joyeuse is stretched out on one of the armchairs—Saint Megrin standing, leaning on the back of another—on the other side D'Epernon is seated at a table with a checkerboard—in the rear—Saint Luc fences with du Halde. Each has near him a page in his colors.

D'EPERNON

Gentlemen, which of you will play chess with me while waiting the return of the King? Saint Megrin will you have your revenge?

SAINT MEGRIN

No, I am distracted today.

JOYEUSE

Oh, decidedly, it's the prediction of the astrologer. True God! He's a true sorcerer. Do you know he indeed predicted that Dugast had only a few days to live, when Queen Marguerite had him assassinated? I bet it's a horoscope of the same sort that's bothering Saint Megrin and that of some great lady of whom he is amorous.

SAINT MEGRIN

(interrupting him excitedly)

Why, you yourself Joyeuse, why don't you play D'Epernon?

JOYEUSE

No thanks.

D'EPERNON

Are you in a reflecting mood as well?

JOYEUSE

On the contrary, so as not to be obliged to reflect.

SAINT LUC

Well, do you want to pass arms with me, Vicomte?

JOYEUSE

That's very fatiguing and then you are not my match. Do a work of charity and help D'Epernon out—

SAINT LUC

So be it!

JOYEUSE

(pulling out a cup and ball from a purse worn at his belt)

Live God, gentlemen, here's a game. This doesn't tire the body or the mind. Do you know this invention has seen a prodigious success at the home of the President? By the way, you weren't there, Saint Luc—what's become of you?

SAINT LUC

I went to see the Italian Players who've obtained permission to perform at the Hotel Bourbon.

JOYEUSE

Ah, yes, charging four sous per person.

SAINT LUC

And then in passing—one moment, D'Epernon. I haven't moved yet.

JOYEUSE

And then, in passing?

SAINT LUC

Where?

JOYEUSE

In passing, you were saying—?

SAINT LUC

Yes, I stopped to watch them lay the first stone of a bridge to be called the Pont Neuf.

D'EPERNON

It's Ducerceau who designed it. They say the King will grant him a patent of nobility.

JOYEUSE

And justice will be done. Do you know that bridge will spare me at least 60-70 steps as I go to the École Saint Germain?

> *(he drops his wallet and calls his page on the other side of the room)*

Bertrand, my wallet.

SAINT LUC

Gentlemen, great news! This morning I was told in confidence the King has abandoned plaited ruffs in favor of Italian lace ruffs.

D'EPERNON

Eh! Why didn't you tell us that? We'll be late a day. See, Saint Megrin knew it.

(to his page)

Tomorrow let me have a lace ruff instead of this one.

SAINT LUC

(laughing)

Ha, ha, you recall that the King exiled you for fifteen days because you were missing a button on your vest?

JOYEUSE

Well, as for me, I am going to exchange news for news, Antraguet is returning today, restored to grace.

SAINT LUC

Really?

JOYEUSE

Yes, he's decidedly one of Guise's adherents. Scarface insisted the King return him his command. For some time the King's been doing whatever he wants.

D'EPERNON

He's the one who needs him. It appears the King of Navarre is in the country, harness on his back.

JOYEUSE

You will see that that damned heretic will make us fight by summer. To put yourself in the country in that heat with fifty pounds of iron on your back, just to come back with a suntan like a Spaniard.

SAINT LUC

That would be a bad tour for you to make, Joyeuse.

JOYEUSE

I confess it. I'm more afraid of heat stroke than a sword stroke and if I could I would fight like Bussy d'Amboise always did in his last duel—by the light of the moon.

SAINT LUC

Has someone news of him?

D'EPERNON

Bussy is still in Anjou near Monsieur. That's one more enemy at least for Guise.

JOYEUSE

Speaking of old Scarface, Saint Megrin, do you know what Marshal de Retz said about him? Said that compared to the Duke of Guise all the princes seem common.

SAINT MEGRIN

Guise, always Guise. Live God! May the occasion present itself.

(drawing his dagger and slashing his glove to pieces)

And by Saint Paul of Bordeaux I intend to hack all the little Lorraine princes like this glove.

JOYEUSE

Bravo, Saint Megrin—true God, I hate them more than you do.

SAINT MEGRIN

More than me! Curses! If that is possible, I would give my title as Count to feel his sword against mine for but five minutes—perhaps that will come.

DU HALDE

Gentlemen, gentlemen, here's Bussy.

SAINT MEGRIN

What! Bussy D'Amboise!

BUSSY D'AMBOISE

Eh, yes, gentlemen, himself, in person—to friends, greetings, hello Saint Megrin.

SAINT MEGRIN

And we thought you were 100 leagues from here.

BUSSY D'AMBOISE

I was three days ago. Today, here I am.

JOYEUSE

Ha, ha, you are then reconciled? He wanted to kill you with Quelus. It wasn't his fault if the blow didn't succeed.

BUSSY D'AMBOISE

Yes, for Madame de Suave—but since then, we measured our swords and they turned out to be of the same length.

SAINT LUC

Speaking of Madame Suave, they say that so that she may be more sure of your fidelity. You wrote her with your blood—as the King did one of his mistresses. Doubtless he was forewarned of your arrival.

BUSSY D'AMBOISE

No. We travelled incognito. But I didn't want to pass so close to you without asking you if there wasn't someone who had need of a second.

SAINT LUC

That might be, if you don't leave us too soon.

BUSSY D'AMBOISE

God's Head! Should the occasion arise, I am the man to delay my departure, so as not to annoy you. It's been so long that nothing's come my way—all the more so, in the provinces one has to look about to be able to fight once a week— Happily I had at hand Saint Phal there. We fought three times because he insisted he'd seen an X on the buttons of a dress whereas I thought they had a Y.

SAINT MEGRIN

Bah! Not possible.

BUSSY D'AMBOISE

Word of honor. Guisard was my second.

JOYEUSE

Who was right?

BUSSY D'AMBOISE

We still don't know yet. The fourth meeting will decide it. But what do I see over there? The pages of d'Antraguet! I thought that since the death of Quelus—

SAINT LUC

The Duke of Guise has solicited his pardon.

BUSSY D'AMBOISE

Ah, yes, solicited—I understand. He's still insolvent, our cousin Guise.

SAINT MEGRIN

Not enough so, yet.

D'EPERNON

True God! You are difficult. I am sure that in the depths of his heart the King is not of your opinion.

SAINT MEGRIN

Let me say one word—

D'EPERNON

Ah, you see he's too busy at the moment. He's learning Latin.

SAINT MEGRIN

God's Head—what does he need Latin for to speak to the French? Let him only say, "Help me, my brave nobility!" And thousands of sharp cutting swords will leave the scabbards they are in. Does he no longer have in his breast the same heart that beat at Jamar and Montcontour—have his perfumed gloves softened his hands to the point they can no longer grasp the belt of a sword?

D'EPERNON

Silence—Saint Megrin. Here he is.

A PAGE

The King.

BUSSY D'AMBOISE

I'm going to hang a big toe outside. I won't show myself until he's in a good mood.

SECOND PAGE

The King.

> *(Everyone rises.)*

THIRD PAGE

The King.

HENRY

(entering)

Greetings, gentlemen, greetings—Villequier, let them inform Madame, my mother of my return and find out if they are bringing my new riding habit. Ah, tell the Queen I will spend the day with her, after setting the day for our departure to Chartres, for you know, gentlemen, that the Queen and I are making a pilgrimage to Notre Dame de Chartres, so as to obtain from Heaven what it has refused us until now—an heir to our crown. Those who wish to follow us will be welcome.

SAINT MEGRIN

Sire, if instead of a pilgrimage, to Chartres, you ordered a campaign in Anjou—if your gentlemen were dressed in armor instead of haircloths and wore swords in the shape of candles, Your Majesty wouldn't lack for penitents, and you would see me in the first rank, sire—if I had to do most of the way on naked feet over hot coals.

HENRY

Each thing will have its turn, my lad. We won't remain behind hand as to what we must do—but at this moment, by God's Grace, our beautiful realm of France is at peace, and the time is not lacking for us to occupy ourselves with our spiritual devotions. Why what do I see? You, at my court, Lord Bussy?

(to Catherine de Medici as she enters)

Come, mother, come: You are going to have news of your beloved son—who, if he had been a submissive brother and respectful subject, would never have left our court.

CATHERINE

He's coming back perhaps, my son.

HENRY

(sitting)

That's what we are going to find out. Sit down, mother. Come forward, Lord Bussy. Where did you leave my brother?

BUSSY D'AMBOISE

In Paris, Sire.

HENRY

In Paris! Would he be in our good city of Paris?

BUSSY D'AMBOISE

No—but he passed through last night.

HENRY

And he's going—

BUSSY D'AMBOISE

To Flanders.

HENRY

You hear that, mother! No doubt we are going to have in our family a Duke of Brabant. And why did he pass so near us without coming to present us his homage of fidelity like a younger son and to his King?

BUSSY D'AMBOISE

Sire, he knows the great friendship that Your Majesty bears him, and he feared that if he once entered the Louvre, you would never let him leave again.

HENRY

And he was right, sir. But at this moment the absence of his good servant and his faithful sword must trouble him. For perhaps rather soon he counts on using it against us. Therefore, Lord Bussy arrange to rejoin him as quickly as possible and leave us even sooner.

(A page enters.)

HENRY

Well—what's wrong?

CATHERINE

My son, doubtless it is Antraguet who is profiting by the permission you voluntarily granted him to reappear at court.

HENRY

Yes, yes—voluntarily! The vile murderer! Mother, my cousin, the Duke of Guise imposes a great sacrifice on me. But for me, God wills that it be complete.

(to page)

Speak!

PAGE

Charles Balzac d'Entragues, Baron of Dunes, Count de Graville, former lieutenant general in the government of Orleans, asks to lay at the feet of Your Majesty the homage of his fidelity and his respect.

HENRY

Yes, yes, now we shall receive our faithful and respectful subject—but before that I wish to give away all that could remind me of that frightful duel. Here Joyeuse, here!

(pulling from his breast a kind of sack)

Here are the earrings Quelus wore—wear them in memory of our common friend. D'Epernon here's Mangiron's gold chain. Saint Megrin, I will give you Schomberg's sword—it was indeed a heavy weight for an eighteen-year-old arm!

HENRY

Let it defend you better than it did him in like circumstances. And now gentlemen, do as I do—don't forget them in your prayers. May God receive in his bosom Quelus, Schomberg and Mangiron. Stay around me, my friends, and sit down—have him enter.

> *(At the sight of d'Entragues, he takes a flask from his purse so he can breathe.)*

HENRY

Come forward here, Baron—and bend the knee— Charles Balzac d'Entragues we have granted you the favor of our royal presence, in the midst of our court— to grant you these.—What we took from you—your dignities and your titles. Rise Baron Dunes, Count of Graville, governor general of our province of Orleans— and receive from our royal person the function you filled before. Arise.

D'ENTRAGUES

No, sire, I shall not rise until Your Majesty publicly acknowledges that my conduct in that funeral duel was that of an honest and honorable knight.

HENRY

Yes—we recognize it for it's the truth. But you dealt some evil blows.

D'ENTRAGUES

And now, Sire, your hand to kiss as a pledge of pardon and forgetfulness.

HENRY

No, no, sir—don't hope for it.

CATHERINE

My son, what are you doing?

HENRY

No, Madame, no—I have been able to pardon him as a Christian—the evil he has done me—but I will never forget it in my life.

ENTRAGUES

Sire, I call time to my aid, time, my fidelity and my submission perhaps it will end by appeasing Your Majesty's wrath.

HENRY

It's possible but your provincial government must need your presence—it has been deprived so long of Baron Dunes—and the well-being of our faithful subjects might suffer—who's making that racket ?

D'EPERNON

Pages belonging to Guise.

HENRY

Our dear cousin from Lorraine doesn't take advantage of the privilege sovereign princes have of appearing before us without being announced. His pages always take care to make enough of a stir so that his arrival will not be a mystery.

SAINT MEGRIN

He treats with Your Majesty as one power to another. He has his subjects as you have yours, and doubtless he's coming armed from head to foot to present in their name a humble request to Your Majesty.

(The Duke enters in complete armor preceded by two pages and followed by four, one of whom bears a box.)

HENRY

Come, Duke, come—someone who's startled by the uproar of your pages are making and who observed you from afar—would bet that you were coming again to beg us to reform some abuse, or to suppress some tax.My people, are a people indeed happy, my dear cousin, to have in you such a tireless representative, and such a patient King in me.

DUKE

It's true that Your Majesty has granted me many favors and I am proud of having so often served as an intermediary between him and his subjects.

SAINT MEGRIN

(aside)

Yes, like a falcon between the huntsman and the game.

DUKE

But today, Sire, a more powerful motive brings me again before Your Majesty, since it is at the same time the interests of your people and your own that I have to discuss.

HENRY

If the affair is so serious, Duke couldn't you attend our next session of the Estates-General? The Three Estates of the nation leave their representatives there and have received our directive to speak to me in the name of their constituents.

DUKE

Your Majesty will be pleased to recall that the sitting has dissolved and won't reassemble until November— when the danger is pressing it seems to me that a privy council.

HENRY

When the danger is pressing—why you terrify us, Duke. Well, all the persons who compose our privy council are here. Speak, Duke, speak.

DUKE

Sire, the course I take with you is bold, perhaps too bold, but to hesitate longer would not be the action of a true and loyal subject.

HENRY

Indeed, sir, indeed.

CATHERINE

My son, allow me to retire.

HENRY

The Duke knows quite well that we have nothing hidden from our august mother—and that in more than one important affair her advice has been useful to us. No, Madame, no.

DUKE

Sire, immense but necessary expenses—since Your Majesty has made them—have exhausted the State Treasury. Until now, Your Majesty with the help of his faithful subjects has found ways to refill it. But this cannot last. The approval of the Holy Father has permitted the alienation of 200,000 of income from the wealth of the clergy. A loan has been forced on members of parliament under the pretext of returning men from foreign wars. The diamonds of the crown are pledged as security for three millions given to Duke Casimir, the money destined as rents for the Hotel de Ville have been misappropriated to another use. And the Estates General have had the audacity to reply by a refusal when Your Majesty proposed to sell crown lands.

HENRY

Yes, yes, Duke, I know our finances are in a bad condition. We will find another superintendent.

DUKE

That measure might be sufficient in time of peace, Sire, but Your Majesty will see himself constrained in time of war. The Huguenots encouraged by your indulgence are making terrifying progress. The King of Navarre has been by the walls of Orleans and the Spanish, profiting by our troubles, have pillaged Anvers, burned 800 houses and put 7,000 inhabitants to the sword.

HENRY

By the living God, if what you tell me is true, we must chastise the Huguenots within and the Spaniards without. We are not afraid of war my handsome cousin. And if need be, we will go ourselves to the tomb of our ancestor Louis IX to seize the flame and we will march at the head of our brave army.

SAINT MEGRIN

And if it is money you lack, Sire, your brave nobles are here to give back to Your Majesty what has come from you. Our houses, our lands, our jewels can be minted, Duke and Live God! By smelting only the braids of our cloaks and monograms of our ladies. we will have wherewithal to send to the enemy for an entire campaign— balls of gold or bullets of money.

HENRY

You hear him, Duke?

DUKE

Yes, Sire, but before this idea came to the Count de Saint Megrin 30,000 of your brave subjects also had it—they've undertaken in writing to furnish money and treasure and men for the army. This was the purpose of the Holy League, sire—and it will be fulfilled, when the moment comes—but I cannot hide from Your Majesty the fears that trouble your faithful subjects in not seeing this great association recognized from on high.

HENRY

And what would that do for it?

DUKE

By naming a leader, Sire, from a great sovereign house, who by his courage and his birth is worthy of confidence and love, and, who, moreover has given enough proof that he is a good Catholic to reassure the zealot of the way he will act in difficult circumstances.

HENRY

By the living God—Duke, I think that your zeal for our royal person is such that you will be ready to spare us the trouble of looking very far for a leader. We will think of it at leisure, my dear cousin, we will think of it at leisure.

DUKE

But, Your Majesty ought to immediately—

HENRY

Duke, when I want to hear a sermon, I will turn Huguenot. Gentlemen, we've busied ourselves enough with affairs of state—let's think a little of our pleasures—I hope that you have received our invitations for this evening and that Your Duchess, and your sister, Madame Montpensier and you, my cousin, will indeed embellish our masked ball.

SAINT MEGRIN

(pointing to the Duke's armor)

Doesn't Your Majesty see that the Duke is already in the costume of one who is searching for adventures.

DUKE

As a redresser of wrongs, Count.

HENRY

Indeed, my handsome cousin, this outfit seems to me a bit hot for the weather.

DUKE

In this weather, a steel helmet is better than a satin winding sheet.

SAINT MEGRIN

The Duke is always hearing an assassin's bullet whistling in his ears.

DUKE

When they strike me in the face, Count—

(pointing to his scar)

here's proof I don't turn to avoid them.

JOYEUSE

(lifting his blow gun)

That's what we're going to find out.

SAINT MEGRIN

(grabbing the peashooter)

Wait! It shall not be said that anyone other than myself shall make the experiment.

(shooting a wad at the Duke's breast)

Here's to you, Duke.

ALL

Bravo! Bravo!

DUKE

(putting his hand on his dagger)

Curses!

SAINT PAUL

(Saint Paul stopping him)

What are you going to do?

HENRY

By the Living God! My cousin, Guise—I would have thought that
beautiful and well made Milanese armor had taken a real shot.

DUKE

You, too, Sire. Make them give respect to the presence of Your
Majesty.

HENRY

Oh, that doesn't matter, Duke, that doesn't matter—act as if we
were not here.

DUKE

Your Majesty allows me to descend to his level?

HENRY

No, Duke, but I can raise him to yours. We will search carefully in
our beautiful kingdom of France for a vacant Duchy to endow our
faithful subject, the Count Saint Megrin.

DUKE

You are master of it, Sire—but from where?

HENRY

Well, we won't make you wait. Count Paul Estueret, we make you
Marquis de Caussade.

DUKE

I am a Duke, Sire.

HENRY

Count Paul Estueret, Marquis de Caussade, we make you Duke
de Saint Megrin—and now Duke answer him for he is your equal.

SAINT MEGRIN

Thanks, Sire, thanks. I have no need of this new favor; and since Your Majesty, is not opposed to it, I intend to defy him in the manner which leads to combat or dishonor—therefore, listen, gentlemen, I, Paul Estueret, Lord of Caussade, Count of Saint Megrin, say to you, Henry of Lorraine, Duke of Guise, taking as witness all those here present, that we defy you to combat to the death, you and all the princes of your house, be it by sword alone, be it by dirk, be it by dagger. So long as heart beats in the body, so long as the blade holds in hand—renouncing in advance your mercy as you must renounce mine—and to this God and Saint Paul aid me!

(throwing down his glove)

To you alone, or to you and others!

D'EPERNON

Bravo, Saint Megrin, well defied!

DUKE

(pointing to the glove)

Saint Paul—!

BUSSY D'AMBOISE

One moment, gentlemen—one moment; I, Louis de Clermont, Lord Bussy d'Amboise, declare myself here sponsor and second to Paul Estueret de Saint Megrin— offering combat to the death to whoever declares themselves sponsor and second to Henry of Lorraine, Duke of Guise—and as a sign of scorn and pledge of combat—here's my glove.

JOYEUSE

Long live God—Bussy you've really committed theft on me, you didn't give me time. But don't worry, if you are killed—

DUKE

Saint Paul— Pick up that glove.

(aside)

You are provoking me too far. Your fate is decided.

(aloud)

Entragues, you will be my second—you, sir, gentlemen, I give you fair play! I am offering you a way of avenging Quelus. Saint Paul, you will prepare my dress sword— it is just the same length as the combat sword of these gentlemen.

SAINT MEGRIN

You are right, Duke, this sword will indeed be too weak to damage armor as prudently solid as that one. But we can go hand to hand, naked to the waist, Duke, and we shall see whose heart still beats.

HENRY

Enough, gentlemen, enough—we will honor the combat by our presence, and we fix it for tomorrow. Now, each of you can claim a gift, and, if it is in our royal power to grant it, you will be satisfied, instantly. What do you want, Saint Megrin?

SAINT MEGRIN

A favorable share of the ground and the sun; for the rest, I trust in God and my sword.

HENRY

And you, Duke, what do you demand?

DUKE

A formal promise before the duel, Your Majesty will recognize the League and name its leader. I've spoken.

HENRY

Although we were not expecting this request, we grant it to you, my dear cousin. Gentlemen, since Milord Guise forces us to it, instead of a masked ball tonight. We shall hold a council of state. I will convoke you all there, gentlemen. As for these two champions, we invite them to profit by this interval, to take good care of the state of their souls. Go, gentlemen. Go.

(They all leave except the King and Catherine de

Medici.)

HENRY

Well, mother, you ought to be satisfied—your two great enemies are going to destroy themselves and you ought to thank me for it, for I authorized a duel which I ought to have prevented.

CATHERINE

Would you have acted so, my son, had you known that one of the conditions of the duel would be to name a leader for the League?

HENRY

No, on my soul, mother. I was expecting a diversion.

CATHERINE

And you've decided?

HENRY

Nothing yet. For the chances of dueling are uncertain. If Guise is killed, well—they'll bury the League with its chief. If he's not— then I will pray God to enlighten me. But in any case, my decision once taken—I warn you in advance—nothing will make me change it. The view from my throne, from time to time, makes me want to be King—and this is one of those times.

CATHERINE

Eh, my son—who more than I desires you to exercise a firm and potent will? The doctor has recommended I rest. And more than ever, I desire not to have any part of the burdens of State.

HENRY

Today, if I'm not wrong, mother, I saw an arm extended towards my throne, covered in iron which wanted to rid me of a share of it, if not all.

CATHERINE

And probably you will grant him what he demands for this leader is demanded by the League using his voice.

HENRY

Yes, yes, I've indeed seen what he pleads for himself—and perhaps mother, I will spare myself real torments by abandoning myself to him! As my brother did after the conspiracy d'Amboise—and yet I don't care for anyone to come petition me armed the way my cousin Guise did. Knees don't bend very well in steel armor.

CATHERINE

And never has your cousin, the Duke, bended his knee before you, but that he has risen, bearing away a piece of your royal cloak.

HENRY

By the Living God. He's never forced our will yet. What we've granted him has always been our own free will and this time again, if we name him head of the League it will be a duty which we impose on him as his master.

CATHERINE

All these duties bring him closer to the throne, my son—and misfortune—misfortune to you if he ever places his foot on the velvet of the first step.

HENRY

What you say there, mother—can you support it by some reasons?

CATHERINE

Do you know what is the purpose of this League you are authorizing?

HENRY

To sustain the altar and the throne.

CATHERINE

At least that's what your cousin Guise said—but from the moment that a subject constitutes himself, by his own authority, defender of the King, my son, he's not far from being a rebel.

HENRY

Could the Duke have such guilty designs?

CATHERINE

The circumstances, at least, accuse him. Alas, my son, I can no longer watch over you as I once did—and yet, perhaps I've once again had the luck of thwarting a conspiracy.

HENRY

A conspiracy! Are they conspiring against me? Speak, speak, mother. What is that paper?

CATHERINE

An agent of the Duke of Guise, the attorney Jean David died at Lyon. His valet was my man—all his papers have been sent to me. This is one of them.

HENRY

Let's see mother, let's see.

(after glancing at it)

A treaty between Don Juan of Austria and the Duke of Guise. A treaty by which they pledge their mutual aid—one to reach the throne of the Netherlands, the other on the throne of France! On the throne of France? What are they planning to do with me, mother?

CATHERINE

See, the last article of the constitution of the League— which is here—not as you know it, my dear Henry, but as it was presented to the Pope—who refused to approve it.

HENRY

(reading)

Then, when the Duke of Guise shall have exterminated the Huguenots, and becomes master of the principal cities of the realm, and all bend under the power of the League, he will bring the King's brother to trial as a manifest abettor of heretics, and after having shaved the King and confirmed him in a monastery— "In a monastery!" They intend to bring me in a monastery?

CATHERINE

Yes, my son—they say that there your last crown awaits you.

HENRY

Mother, would the Duke dare this?

CATHERINE

Consider history—Pepin founded a dynasty—and what did he give his King in return for the royal mantle?

HENRY

A sackcloth, mother, a sackcloth. I know it—but times have changed—to reach the throne of France, you must be born so as to have certain rights.

CATHERINE

Can't they be invented. See this family tree?

HENRY

The House of Lorraine goes back to Charlemagne? It doesn't. You know very well, it doesn't.

CATHERINE

You see measures have been taken so it will be believed that it does.

HENRY

Ah, cousin Guise, you have a terrible grudge against our beautiful French crown. Mother, can't he be punished for daring to pretend to it without our permission?

CATHERINE

I understand you, my son—it's not enough to cut him—he needs to be sewn up.

HENRY

But he's fighting tomorrow with Saint Megrin—Saint Megrin is brave and skillful.

CATHERINE

Do you think the Duke is less brave and less skillful than he?

HENRY

Mother, if we were to bless the sword of Saint Megrin.

CATHERINE

If the Duke has his blessed, my son—

HENRY

You are right. But who could prevent me from naming Saint Megrin chief of the League.

CATHERINE

And who will recognize him? Does he have a party? Perhaps there might be a way to manage everything, my son, but it requires resolve.

HENRY

(hesitating)

Resolve!

CATHERINE

Yes—be King—the Duke will become a submissive subject if not respectful. I know him better than you, Henry—-he is strong because you are weak—under his apparent energy he hides an irresolute character. It's a need printed in iron. Lean on him, he'll bend.

HENRY

Yes, yes, he'll bend. But what is the way? Let's see— must they both be exiled? I am prepared to sign their exile.

CATHERINE

No—perhaps I have another way. But swear to me—in the future you will consult me before them on all you plan to do.

HENRY

Is that all, mother? I swear it.

CATHERINE

My son—oaths pronounced before the altar are more agreeable to God.

HENRY

And bind men, better right? Well, come, mother, I abandon myself completely to you.

CATHERINE

Yes, my son—let's go to the chapel.

CURTAIN

ACT III

SCENE 3

The Chapel of the Duchess of Guise.

MME de COSSE

(placing a black domino on a table)

Can you imagine, Marie, the Duchess wants to go to a court ball in a simple hood?

MARIE

(placing flowers on the same table)

That's because the Duchess is not a flirt.

LA CHAPPELLE-MARTEAU

But without being a flirt, she can show some of her charms. What's the good of being pretty and well built if you cover your face in this black mask and envelope your body in this which is big enough to be the dress of a hermit? Why not dress like Diana or Hebe?

ARTHUR

She's the one who wanted you to arrange this costume, Madame de Cosse.

MME de COSSE

See this little dandy! Go bring your mistress' fan on the train for her dress and don't talk about her dress. You still know nothing about it. In three or four years— fine!

ARTHUR

Heavens! I'm going to be fifteen.

MME de COSSE

Fourteen, my handsome page, by your leave.

MARIE

Anyway, this domino is only to enter in the ball room. A party of women, you know, only wear masks for the first few glances and then reappear in regular dress.

MME de COSSE

And that's wrong. In the past, one kept one's disguise for the entire night. For example, at the famous masked ball for the coronation of Henry II twenty-five years ago. I was only twenty.

ARTHUR

It was thirty years ago, Mme de Cosse, by your leave.

MME de COSSE

Twenty-five or thirty—little matter. Then I was fifteen, well, everyone remained in costume, until the astronomer, Lucas Gaudire, predicted the King would die in combat. Eleven years later it happened—just as it was predicted.

ARTHUR

It's very unfortunate. Since that time there haven't been any more tournaments.

MME de COSSE

Indeed, it's something really annoying. It would be nice to see young men of your age joust. They are effeminate dandies compared to the Knights of Henry the II.

ARTHUR

You might even say, of the Knights of King Francis the First—you've seen them, Madame de Cosse.

MME de COSSE

I was a child, I can't recall it. A child in the cradle, do you hear?

MARIE

But it seems to me, Madame, that Baron D'Epernon, the Vicomte Joyeuse, the Lord de Bussy, Baron Dunes—

ARTHUR

And the Count de Saint Megrin—too—

MME de COSSE

Ah, there you go again with your little Saint Megrin—I would like to have seen him in armor weighing 200 pounds, like my noble husband used to wear when he crowned me lady of love and beauty and in my honor broke five lances, which your Saint Megrin couldn't move with both hands. It was at the famous tournament of Soissons.

MARIE

At the famous tournament of Soissons?

ARTHUR

Yes, at the famous tournament of Soissons in 1546, a year before the death of Francis I, when Mme Cosse was still in the cradle.

MME de COSSE

Little wiseacre! You are really bold because you are related to the Duchess.

ARTHUR

(running to the Duchess who enters)

Oh, come, my beautiful cousin and mistress and protect me against the wrath of your first lady of honor.

DUCHESS

(distracted)

What have you done? Another prank?

ARTHUR

Discourteous as I am, I remember dates.

MME de COSSE

(interrupting him)

Madame seems preoccupied.

DUCHESS

Me? No, you wouldn't have found a handkerchief with my coat of arms?

MARIE

No, Madame.

ARTHUR

I'm going to find it, and if I find it what will be my reward?

DUCHESS

Your reward child? Does a handkerchief deserve a great reward? Well, look for it, Arthur.

MARIE

While you were retired in your apartment resting, Queen Louise came to pay a visit. She had the cutest little monkey.

MME de COSSE

Yes, she wanted to know what costume you planned to wear—she went to Madame Montpensier, and as I was there, I know all the costumes of the lords and ladies of the court.

DUCHESS

(to Arthur who has returned to sit at her feet)

Well?

ARTHUR

I couldn't find it.

MME de COSSE

Joyeuse is coming as Alcibiades. He has a massive golden helmet. His costume they say cost him 10,000 pounds. M' D'Epernon is—

ARTHUR

And Saint Megrin—

(The Duchess trembles.)

MME de COSSE

Ha! Saint Megrin? He also has a very brilliant costume—but today he ordered another one, quite simple. The costume of an astrologer, similar to that worn by Cosimo Ruggière.

DUCHESS

Ruggière? Tell me, doesn't Ruggière live in the Rue Grenelle near the Hotel Soissons?

MARIE

Yes.

DUCHESS

(aside)

No more doubt! It was at his place! I thought I recognized it.

(aloud)

Did no one else come?

MME de COSSE

Yes, the Abbé Brantome to offer you a copy of his Gallant Ladies—I placed a copy on the table. The Queen of Navarre plays a
major role in it. Navarre plays a major role in it. And then the poet,
Ronsard— he absolutely insisted on seeing you—You reproached
him the other day for not taking sufficient care of his verse—so
he's brought you a small specimen.

DUCHESS

Rhymes?

MME de COSSE

No, Madame, but better done than he usually does. Do you wish
to hear them?

DUCHESS

Give it to Arthur—he will read it.

ARTHUR

(reading)

Mignonne, go examine the rose which opened this morning—

> *Its purple dress in the sun*
> *Not having yet been ruined at vespers.*
> *The folds of its purple dress*
> *And its complexion so much like yours.*
>
> *Alas, see how a short time span*
> *Mignonne—it has up above.*

Alas, alas, its beauties left to fall
O truly cruel nature
Since such a flower does not last
Except from morn to midnight.

There listen, Mignonne
While your age is flowering
In its plushest green novelty
Gather, gather, your youth like this flowers
Age will tarnish your beauty.

DUCHESS

(always distracted)

But it seems those verses are good—

ARTHUR

Oh, Saint Megrin has written some at least as pretty.

DUCHESS

Saint Megrin.

MME de COSSE

Still, these are not love poems.

ARTHUR

And why's that?

MME de COSSE

It's likely that he has not yet found any woman worthy of his love, since he is the only one, among all the young men of the court who does not wear the arms of his lady on his cloak.

ARTHUR

And if he loved someone whose arms he could not wear? Perhaps that's it.

DUCHESS

Yes—perhaps that's it.

MME de COSSE

(to Arthur)

Why—what's so remarkable about this little Count Saint Megrin, for him to be the object of your enthusiasm?

ARTHUR

So remarkable? Ah, all I ask is to be worthy of becoming his page if I can no longer be one of my beautiful cousin's.

DUCHESS

You love him then?

ARTHUR

If I were a woman, I wouldn't have any other knight.

DUCHESS

(excitedly)

Ladies, I can finish my toilet by myself—I will call you back if I need you. Stay, Arthur, I have some commissions to give you.

(The women leave.)

ARTHUR

I await your orders.

DUCHESS

There are none. Why I no longer know what I wanted to order you—I am distracted, preoccupied—how bizarre you are with your fanaticism for the young Vicomte Joyeuse.

ARTHUR

Joyeuse! No—Saint Megrin.

DUCHESS

Oh, yes—that's right—but what do you find so extraordinary in that young man?

ARTHUR

You haven't seen him first with the King?

DUCHESS

Yes—

ARTHUR

And who could you compare him to for skill? If he mounts a horse, that horse is always the most fiery— if he fights less often than the others, it's because his strength is known—and people hesitate to quarrel with him. The King alone, perhaps, would defend himself against him. All our young Lords of the court envy him, and even the cut of their vest and cloak is always modeled on his.

DUCHESS

Yes, yes, that's true—he's a man of good taste—but Madame de Cosse spoke so coldly for the ladies, and you wouldn't want to take as your ideal a chevalier the ladies didn't like.

ARTHUR

Lady de Sauve is there to witness the contrary.

DUCHESS

(excitedly)

Lady de Suave—they say he never loved her.

ARTHUR

If he no longer loves her, he is certainly in love with another.

DUCHESS

Could he have chosen you for his confidant? It wouldn't argue for his prudence, choosing one so young.

ARTHUR

If I was his confidant, my beautiful cousin, they could sooner kill me than tear his secret form me. But he's confided nothing to me. I've simply observed.

DUCHESS

You've observed—what—what have you observed?

ARTHUR

You remember the day when the King invited the whole court to visit the lions that he'd just brought from Tunisia and had placed in the Louvre with those that had grown up there?

DUCHESS

Oh, yes—their appearance alone frightened me although I was viewing them form a gallery at least ten feet above them.

ARTHUR

Well, hardly had we left than their keepers let out a shout. I went back in. Saint Megrin had just rushed into the animal's enclosure to gather a bouquet which a lady had let fall.

DUCHESS

The wretch! That was my bouquet.

ARTHUR

Your's my beautiful cousin?

DUCHESS

Did I say mine? Yes, mine or that of Madame de Suave. You know he's desperately loved by Mme de Suave. The fool! And what did he do with that bouquet?

ARTHUR

Oh! He placed it passionately against his mouth, he pressed it against his heart. The keeper opened a gate and made him leave almost by force. He laughed like a madman, threw him money, then he noticed me, and hid the bouquet in his breast, leapt on his horse which was waiting in the court of the Louvre and disappeared.

DUCHESS

Is that all? Is that all? Oh, once more, once more! Tell me about him again!

ARTHUR

And after I saw him, he—

DUCHESS

Silence, child! The Duke—stay near me, Arthur, don't leave me unless I tell you to.

(Enter the Duke.)

DUKE

You were getting up, Madame. Are you going to go back in your apartment?

DUCHESS

No, Milord, I was going to call my women for my toilette.

DUKE

It's unnecessary, Madame. The ball won't take place— and you ought to be happy about it; you seemed to be going unwillingly.

DUCHESS

I was following your orders—ad I did what I could so you wouldn't notice it was painful for me.

DUKE

What do you want! I understood that this reclusion to which you condemn yourself is ridiculous at your age—and that from time to time you must show yourself at court. Certain persons, Madame, might notice your absence and attribute motives to it— but there's another matter, Madame. Arthur leave me.

DUCHESS

And why send the child away, sir—do you want a secret conversation?

DUKE

And why keep him, Madame? Are you afraid to remain alone with me?

DUCHESS

Me, sir—and why?

DUKE

In that case, leave Arthur. Well?

ARTHUR

I am awaiting the orders of my mistress, milord.

DUKE

You hear him?

DUCHESS

Arthur—go away.

ARTHUR

I obey.

(Arthur leaves.)

DUKE

True God! Madame it is bizarre, that your orders given through my mouth need to be ratified by yours.

DUCHESS

That young man belongs to me and he thought it his duty to wait for orders from myself.

DUKE

That obstinacy is not natural, Madame—you know Henry of Lorraine, and you know that he always charges his dagger with repeating orders from his mouth.

DUCHESS

Eh, see—what conclusions could you draw from that child's obedience or lack thereof?

DUKE

Me? None. But I needed his absence to explain to you more freely the motive that brought me. Would you be willing to act as my secretary?

DUCHESS

Me, sir. And to write to whom?

DUKE

What does it matter to you? I will dictate.

(bringing pen and paper)

Here's what you need.

DUCHESS

I fear not to be able to form a single word—my hand trembles. Couldn't you get someone else?

DUKE

No, Madame—it is indispensable that it be you.

DUCHESS

But at least, put it off till later.

DUKE

It cannot be put off—anyway, it suffices that your writing be legible. Write then—

DUCHESS

I am ready.

DUKE

(dictating)

Several members of the Holy League will gather tonight at the Hotel de Guise. The doors will remain open until one in the morning—you can, with the help of the League's costume pass without being noticed. The apartment of the Duchess de Guise is on the third floor.

DUCHESS

I won't write any more until I know who this letter is destined for.

DUKE

I will show you, Madame, in putting on the address.

DUCHESS

It cannot be for you, sir, and to all others it compromises my honor.

DUKE

Your honor? Long, live God—Madame—and who ought to be more jealous than myself? Let me judge— and follow my desire.

DUCHESS

Your desire? I must refuse my own.

DUKE

Then obey my orders.

DUCHESS

Your orders. Perhaps I have the right to demand the reason.

DUKE

The reason, Madame. All these delays prove to me that you know the reason.

DUCHESS

Me? And how?

DUKE

Little matter! Write.

DUCHESS

Allow me to return—

DUKE

You shall not leave.

DUCHESS

You will obtain nothing from me by constraining me to remain.

DUKE

(forcing her to sit)

Perhaps you will consider, Madame—my orders scorned by you are not yet scorned by all the world and with a word I can substitute for the elegant chapel of the Hotel de Guise a humble cell in a nunnery.

DUCHESS

Designate the convent where I must retire, Duke, the wealth I brought you as a Princess of Porcian will pay the dowry of the Duchess of Guise.

DUKE

Yes, Madame, you judge in yourself what would only be a weak penitence. Anyway, hope will follow you despite the gates. Are not walls erected so high they cannot be pierced if someone is helped by an adroit knight, powerful and devoted? No, Madame, no—I won't allow you that chance. But let's return to that letter; it needs to be finished.

DUCHESS

Never, sir, never!

DUKE

Don't push me to the last extremity, Madame. It's too much already that I've consented to threaten you twice.

DUCHESS

Well, I prefer an eternal seclusion.

DUKE

Death and damnation! Do you think I have only one means?

DUCHESS

And what other do you have?

(the Duke pours the contents of a flask in a cup)

Ah, you want to murder me—what are you doing, sir, what are you doing?

DUKE

Nothing. I only hope that the sight of this brew will have strength my words lack.

DUCHESS

Ah, what! Could you? Ah—

DUKE

Write, Madame, write.

DUCHESS

No, no. Oh, my God! My God!

DUKE

(seizing the cup)

Well—?

DUCHESS

Henry, in the name of God! I am innocent—I swear it—may the death of a weak woman not soil your name. Henry this would be a horrible crime, for I am not guilty—I embrace your knees—what more do you want? Yes, yes, I fear death.

DUKE

There's one way to escape.

DUCHESS

It's more frightful still. But no, all this is only a crime to frighten me—you couldn't have, you haven't had this execrable idea.

DUKE

(laughing)

A game, Madame.

DUCHESS

No—your smile has told me everything—let me have a minute to recuperate.

(she puts her head in her hands and prays)

DUKE

A moment, Madame—only a moment.

DUCHESS

(after meditating)

And now, oh, my God! have pity on me!

DUKE

Have you decided?

DUCHESS

(rising)

I have.

DUKE

To obey.

DUCHESS

(taking the cup)

To the death!

DUKE

(tearing the cup from her and throwing it on the ground)

You love him a lot, Madame—she prefers—curses! Curses on you and on him. Especially on him—who is loved so much—write.

DUCHESS

Misfortune! Woe is me!

DUKE

Yes, misfortune—for it is much easier for a woman to die than to suffer—

(seizing her arm with his iron glove)

Write.

DUCHESS

Oh—leave me alone.

DUKE

Write.

DUCHESS

(trying to release her arm)

You are hurting me, Henry.

DUKE

Write, I tell you.

DUCHESS

You are hurting me a lot, Henry. You are hurting me terribly—mercy! mercy! Ah!

DUKE

Then write.

DUCHESS

Can I do it? My sight troubles me—a cold sweat—my God, I thank you—I am going to die.

(she faints)

DUKE

Eh? No, Madame.

DUCHESS

What do you demand from me?

DUKE

That you obey me—

DUCHESS

(overwhelmed)

Yes, yes, I will obey. My God! You know I have braved death—
sorrow alone has conquered me—it is greater than my strength.
You have allowed it, O my God— the rest is in your hands.

DUKE

(dictating)

The apartment of the Duchess of Guise is on the third floor and this
key opens the door. The address now.

> *(as he folds the letter, the Duchess pulls back her sleeve
> and bruises can be seen on her arm)*

DUCHESS

What would the nobility of France say if it knew the Duke of Guise
bruised the arm of his wife with a Knights gauntlet?

DUKE

The Due of Guise would give an account to whoever asked him—
finish; to Monsieur, the Count of Saint Megrin.

DUCHESS

So it really was for him.

DUKE

Didn't you guess it?

DUCHESS

Sir, my conscience allows me to doubt it, at least.

DUKE

Enough! Enough! Call one of your pages and send him the letter.

(going to the door and taking the key)

And this key.

DUCHESS

Ah, sir, cannot you have more pity on yourself than you have had on me?

DUKE

Call a page!

DUCHESS

No one is there.

DUKE

Arthur, your favorite page mustn't be far off—call him, I order you to do it—call him—but above all, Madame, pay careful attention that I am here behind this screen. One sign, one word—that child is dead—and it will be you who killed him.

(he whistles)

Think about it, Madame.

DUCHESS

(calling)

Arthur.

ARTHUR

(entering)

Here I am Madame, God—great God—how pale you are!

DUCHESS

Me, pale? No, no—you are mistaken.

(offering him the letter and pulling it back)

It's nothing—go away, Arthur, go away.

ARTHUR

Leave you alone when you are ill? Shall I call your women?

DUCHESS

Be careful of yourself, Arthur! Take this letter—this key—and go—leave! Leave!

ARTHUR

(reading)

Oh, the Count Saint Megrin! Oh—how happy he will be, Madame—I run—

(he leaves)

DUCHESS

Happy! Oh, no, no come back—come back—Arthur! Arthur!

DUKE

(emerging and placing his hand over her mouth)

Silence, Madame.

DUCHESS

(falling in his arms)

Ah!

DUKE

(pulling her into the room and locking it with a double lock)

And now let this door not reopen for anyone except for him.

C U R T A I N

ACT IV

SCENE 5

Same as Act II.

ARTHUR

In the hall of the council, the apartment of the Count de Saint Me-grin—on the left.

(Saint Megrin emerges from his apartment)

For you, Count.

SAINT MEGRIN

This letter and this key are for me, you say? Yes "The Count Saint Megrin"—from whom did you get this?

ARTHUR

Although you couldn't have expected them from anyone—couldn't you hope to get them from someone?

SAINT MEGRIN

From someone? What? And who are you?

ARTHUR

Are you so ignorant in heraldry, count that you cannot recognize that the united arms of two sovereigns houses?

SAINT MEGRIN

The Duchess of Guise.

(putting his hand, Arthur's mouth)

Shut up—I know everything. She herself sent this letter by you?

ARTHUR

She herself—

SAINT MEGRIN

She herself! Young man don't try to trick me—I don't know her writing—admit to me, you tried to deceive me.

ARTHUR

Me—deceive you? Ah—!

SAINT MEGRIN

From where did she send this letter?

ARTHUR

From her chapel.

SAINT MEGRIN

She was alone?

ARTHUR

Alone.

SAINT MEGRIN

And how did she seem to feel?

ARTHUR

I don't know, but she was pale and trembling.

SAINT MEGRIN

In her chapel! Alone, pale and trembling. All this must be—yet I was far from expecting it.

(rereading it)

Several members of the Holy League will meet tonight at the Hotel de Guise. The doors remain open until one in the morning—with the help of the disguise of a Leaguer, you can pass without being noticed. The apartment of the Duchess is on the third floor—and this key opens her door. To the Count of Saint Megrin. It's really for me—for me—it's not a dream—my head is not distracted—this key—this paper—these written lines—everything is real. It's not an illusion.

ARTHUR

In your turn, Count, silence!

SAINT MEGRIN

Yes, you are right—silence, and to you, too, young man, silence! Be mute as the tomb! Forget what you have done— what you have seen—don't remember my name—don't remember the name of your mistress. She's shown prudence in charging you with this message—it's not among children one must fear informers.

ARTHUR

And as for me, Count, I am proud to have a secret between us.

SAINT MEGRIN

Yes, but a terrible secret—one of those secrets which kill. Ah, be careful that your face does not betray, that your eyes never reveal it—you are young. Preserve the gaiety and carelessness of your age. If it should happen that we should meet—pass without recognizing me, without noticing me—if in the future you should again have something to apprise me of—don't express it in words—don't confine it to paper—a sign, a look, will tell me all—I will grasp the least of your gestures I will understand your most secret thought. I cannot reward you for the joy I owe you—but if ever you have need of my aid or help—come to me, speak and whatever you ask, you shall have it—on my soul—be it my blood—Leave, leave now, and make sure no one sees you. Goodbye! Goodbye!

ARTHUR

(pressing his hand)

Goodbye, count, goodbye.

(exit Arthur)

SAINT MEGRIN

Go, young man—and may heaven watch over you. Ah, I am loved. But it is ten o'clock and I hardly have time to obtain the costume—Georges—Georges—

(his valet appears)

I must have a Leaguer's costume tonight: Busy yourself instantly with obtaining it. Let me have it here, when I need it.—Go—

(Georges leaves)

But who's coming here?

(enter Ruggière)

Ah, it's you, Cosimo Ruggière. Come, oh, come, Father, that I may thank you. Well, all your predictions have been realized. I thank you—for I am happy—more happy than you can know. You are responding to me, you are examining me.

RUGGIÈRE

(escorting him towards the light)

Young man, come with me.

SAINT MEGRIN

Oh—what can you read in my face—except a future of love and joy?

RUGGIÈRE

Death, perhaps—

SAINT MEGRIN

What are you saying, father?

RUGGIÈRE

Death!

SAINT MEGRIN

(laughing)

Ah! Father, mercy—just let me live until tomorrow, it's all that I ask of you.

RUGGIÈRE

My son, recall Dugast.

SAINT MEGRIN

Dugast! It is true, that I run a danger—tomorrow—I fight with the Duke of Guise.

RUGGIÈRE

Tomorrow—at what time?

SAINT MEGRIN

At ten o'clock.

RUGGIÈRE

It's not that. If tomorrow, you see still the light of heaven, count on long and happy life.

(going to the window)

Do you see that star?

SAINT MEGRIN

Which shines near another more brilliant still?

RUGGIÈRE

Yes, and to the west, do you see that dark cloud which is only a point in infinity?

SAINT MEGRIN

Yes—well?

RUGGIÈRE

Well, in an hour that star will have disappeared behind that cloud, and that star—it's yours.

(he leaves)

SAINT MEGRIN

That star—is mine—Ruggière—stop! He doesn't hear me—he's going to the Queen Mother. That star is mine—and that cloud! Long Live God! I am indeed foolish to believe the words of that visionary—these things have never deceived him, he says—Dugast, Dugast! And you, too, you wanted, as I do, a love rendezvous when you fell murdered and your blood pouring from you twenty-two wounds, boiling still with hope and joy. Ah if I too must die, My God, My God!, let me die at least after I return.

(Enter Joyeuse.)

JOYEUSE

I was looking for you, Saint Megrin. Well, what are you doing there? Are you reading in the stars?

SAINT MEGRIN

Me? No.

JOYEUSE

I took you for an astrologer as I entered. What? Again? Why what's wrong with you?

SAINT MEGRIN

Nothing, nothing—I'm looking at the heavens.

JOYEUSE

It is superb. The stars are sparkling.

SAINT MEGRIN

(with melancholy)

Joyeuse, do you think that after our death our soul must live in one of those bright spheres on which our sight stopped once during our lives?

JOYEUSE

Those thoughts never come to me, in my soul; they are too sad. You know my slogan: Be hilarious, joyously—! So much for this world. As for the next, little matter to me what it will be, so long as I am all right.

SAINT MEGRIN

(without listening to him)

Do you think that we will be united with persons we have loved here? Speak: Do you think that one can be happy in eternity?

JOYEUSE

True God—you are going crazy, Saint Megrin—what the devil language are you talking to me in? Manage for yourself so that tomorrow at the same hour. The Duke de Guise can give you sure news and don't ask that of me. I've already dislocated me neck from looking in the air.

SAINT MEGRIN

You are right! Yes, I am foolish.

JOYEUSE

Here's the King—look, get rid of this troubled air— one would say, on my soul, that this duel worried you. Are you angry?

SAINT MEGRIN

Me, angry? True God! If he kills me, Joyeuse, it won't be my life that I regret, it will be leaving him his.

(King Henry, Epernon, Saint Luc, Bussy, Du Halde and others enter.)

HENRY

At ease, gentlemen, at ease. All our measures are taken. Lord de Bussy we return our friendship to you, in reward for the manner in which you have seconded our brave subject, the Count de Saint Megrin.

BUSSY

Sire!

HENRY

(to Saint Megrin)

There you are, my worthy friend—why didn't you come to see me? Gentlemen, my mother will assist at the sitting—inform her that it's going to open. Ah, first of all—on the first step place a stool for the Count Saint Megrin.

(to Saint Megrin)

I have to speak to you—by the Living God—here we are all assembled, gentlemen—the only one missing is our dear cousin de Guise.

CATHERINE

(entering)

No need to wait, my son. I noticed his pages in the antechamber.

HENRY

They will be welcome, mother. Gentlemen take your places. Epernon, yours is at the table—you will be our secretary.

CATHERINE

Above all, sire—

HENRY

Don't worry, mother—don't worry—you have my word.

(The Duke of Guise enters.)

HENRY

Enter, my dear cousin, enter. We thought at first to have prepared the act of recognition we had promised, but then we thought that the one the Governor of Peronne made the nobles of that city sign would be better. As far as the nomination of the leader of the league— mention a bit further down would suffice, and already, you have without doubt some ideas for its drawing up.

DUKE

Yes, sir, I am busy with it. I wanted to spare Your Majesty the trouble—the boredom.

HENRY

You are indeed amiable, cousin. Would you give this act to Baron d'Epernon—read it to us aloud in an intelligible voice, Baron. Now, listen, gentlemen.

D'EPERNON

(reading)

An association made between the princes, lords, gentlemen, and others about the ecclesiastical constitution of Picardy—first—

HENRY

Wait, Epernon. Gentlemen, we all know this act, which I have shown you a copy— therefore there's no need to read the twenty-six articles of which it is composed— pass to the end, and you Duke—approach and dictate yourself—consider that it's a question of naming the head of a great association. The chief must necessarily have great powers. Now, my dear cousin, do as well.

DUKE

I thank you for your confidence, Sire, you will be satisfied.

SAINT MEGRIN

What are you doing, Sire?

HENRY

Leave me alone.

DUKE

First, the man that His Majesty will honor with his choice must be the issue of a sovereign house, worthy of the love and of the confidence of the French, through his past conduct, and his fidelity to the Catholic religion.

Second, the Title of Lieutenant General of the Kingdom of France will be granted and troops placed at his disposal.

Third, as his actions will have for this end the greatest good for the cause, he must account for his actions only to God and his conscience.

HENRY

Very good.

SAINT MEGRIN

Good—and you can approve such unheard of conditions, Sire—and clothe one man with such power?

HENRY

Silence!

JOYEUSE

But, Sire!

HENRY

Silence, gentlemen, we desire, do you hear, we desire positively that whoever we are going to choose, it will be agreeable to you. Cousin, give me then, as a good and honest subject, an example of submission. You are the first person in my kingdom after me—my dear cousin, and in this case, especially, you are interested that they obey me.

DUKE

Sire, I recognize in advance as chief of the Holy League, whoever you shall designate, and I will regard as a rebel whoever dares defy his orders.

HENRY

That's just fine, Duke. Write Epernon.

(rising before his throne)

We, Henry of Valois, by the grace of God, King of France and Poland approve by the present act, dictated by our faithful and loving cousin, Henry of Lorraine, Duke of Guise—the association known under the name of the Holy League—and by our authority we declare ourselves its leader.

DUKE

What?

HENRY

In proof of which we have set our royal seal.

(stepping from the throne and taking the pen)

And have signed it with our hand.
Henry of Valois.

(passing the pen to the Duke)

You next my cousin, as you are first in the kingdom after me—well, you hesitate? Do you think that Henry of Valois and the true Fleur de lys of France doesn't look as worthy as Henry of Lorraine and three little blackbirds. By the living God—you wanted a man who possessed the love of the French? Aren't we loved, Duke? Answer from your heart. You wanted a man of high nobility. I think I'm as good a gentlemen as any here—sign, sir, sign for you have already said, that whoever does not sign will be a rebel.

DUKE

(to the Queen Mother, aside)

O Catherine! Catherine!

HENRY

(pointing to where Guise must sign)

Here, Duke, just below mine.

JOYEUSE

Long live God! I wasn't expecting this.

(offering to take the pen)

After you, sir.

HENRY

Yes, gentlemen, sign, all sign. Epernon, you will see to it that copies of this Act are sent to all provinces of our kingdom.

D'EPERNON

Yes, Sire.

SAINT PAUL

(in a low voice to the Duke)

We haven't been lucky in our first enterprise.

DUKE

(low)

Fortune owes us compensation. The second will succeed. Mayenne has arrived. You will follow his orders.

HENRY

Gentlemen, we really ask your pardon for this long session, it hasn't been quite as amusing as a masked ball, but, blame our dear cousin, Guise—he was the one who forced it on us. Goodbye, Duke, goodbye. Continue always to watch over the needs of the State, as a good and faithful subject, as you've just done, and don't forget that whoever refuses obedience to the leader I have named will be declared guilty of high treason. On that I abandon you to the care of God, gentlemen—are you satisfied with me, Mother ?

CATHERINE

Yes, my son, but don't forget that it was I—

HENRY

No, no, mother; anyway. You'll make sure I don't forget, won't you?

SAINT MEGRIN

(aside)

She's waiting for me, and the King has told me to stay.

(All leave except Henry and Saint Megrin.)

HENRY

Well, Saint Megrin, I've profited I hope by your advice, I've dethroned my cousin Guise and here I am King of the League in his place.

SAINT MEGRIN

May you not repent of it, Sire. But this idea was not yours. I recognize in it—

HENRY

Well, what? Speak.

SAINT MEGRIN

The political craftiness of your mother. She believes she's gained everything when she's gained time. I suspect that she's plotting something against the Duke. I've heard her in speaking of him, call him her friend— as for you, Sire, it's with regret that I saw you sign the act. You were King, now you are only a leader of a party.

HENRY

What else was there to do?

SAINT MEGRIN

Repress the Florentine power politics and act frankly.

HENRY

In what manner?

SAINT MEGRIN

As King—Long live God—proofs of the rebellion of the Duke of Guise would not have been lacking.

HENRY

I had them.

SAINT MEGRIN

Then you must use them and put him on trial.

HENRY

The Parliaments are for him.

SAINT MEGRIN

You must impose on the Parliaments the power of your will. The Bastille has strong walls, a faithful governor and the Duke in being placed there would only be following in the steps of Marshals Montmorency and De Cosse.

HENRY

My friend, there are no walls solid enough to shut in such a prisoner. I know only a lead coffin and a marble tomb can answer to me for that, just put him in the state to enter one, Saint Megrin—and I will take on myself to smelt one and to erect the other.

SAINT MEGRIN

And that being done, Sire, he will be punished, but not as he deserves.

HENRY

Little matter to me the difference in means so long as the result is the same. I hope Saint Megrin, that you have not neglected to prepare yourself for this duel.

SAINT MEGRIN

No, Sire, but as yet, I have not had time to accomplish my religious duties.

HENRY

What do you mean, you haven't had time? Have you forgotten the duel with Jarnac and Chataigneraie? It was fixed for fifteen days after the challenge. Well, for fifteen days, Jarnac spent them in prayer while La Chataigneraie ran from pleasure to pleasure—without any other thought of God. So, God punished him, Saint Megrin.

SAINT MEGRIN

Sire, my intention is to accomplish all my duties as a Christian, but above all there are others which call me—allow me—

HENRY

What do you mean, others?

SAINT MEGRIN

Sire, my life is in God's hands. And if he decides my death, His will be done.

HENRY

Hey, what's that you say—sir—your life—does it belong to you, sir, to make so little of the matter? No, by the living God! It belongs to us, your King and friend. When it's a question of your own business, you are allowed to kill yourself, if such is your good pleasure—but when it's a question of ours, Count, we pray you to think twice about it.

SAINT MEGRIN

True-God, Sire, I will do my best, be easy.

HENRY

You will do your best. That's not enough. Make him swear that he has neither breastplate nor talisman, nor hidden weapons, and when he has done so, then recall all your strength, all your courage, rush hard on him.

SAINT MEGRIN

Yes, Sire.

HENRY

Once delivered from him, you see, we are no longer two in France, I am truly, King—truly free—my mother is going to be proud of the advice she gave me—for you are right, it came from her—and I have to pay for it with obedience. But, after your victory, she will no longer have any way to control me—Besides, you will protect me against her—you are my friend.

SAINT MEGRIN

Sire, God and my sword will help me.

HENRY

Your sword—I want to judge it myself.

(calling)

Du Halde—bring duelling swords.

SAINT MEGRIN

Sire, at such an hour when Your Majesty must need repose?

HENRY

Repose! Repose! They all talk to me of repose! Do you think he's asleep? Him? Or if he sleeps, what's he dreaming? Let him command insolently on the throne of France and as for me—me, his King—I can pray humbly in a cloister. A King never sleeps, Saint Megrin.

(calling)

Du Halde, give us those swords.

SAINT MEGRIN

The hour slips away; she's expecting me.

(aloud)

Sire, this is impossible for me—you have reminded me of sacred duties; it's necessary that I accomplish them.

HENRY

Well, listen tomorrow.

(the clock strikes)

Wait, I think it's midnight.

SAINT MEGRIN

Yes, Sir, it's midnight.

HENRY

Each time that hour strikes I pray God to bless the day that is beginning—I have to leave you—but come find me tomorrow before the duel—Du Halde bring the swords to my room.

SAINT MEGRIN

I shall go, Sire, I shall go.

HENRY

Fine, I am counting on you.

SAINT MEGRIN

Now, I can withdraw, Your Majesty, is satisfied.

HENRY

Yes, the King is so happy, that as a friend he wants to do something for you—here, here's a talisman, on which Ruggière has pronounced charms—he who wears it cannot die by steel or by fire. I am loaning it to you— you will return it to me after the combat.

SAINT MEGRIN

Yes, Sire.

HENRY

Goodbye, Saint Megrin.

SAINT MEGRIN

Goodbye, Sire, goodbye.

(The King leaves.)

SAINT MEGRIN

Finally, I am alone.

(calling)

Georges—ah, there you are! My costume! Fine—help me—help me. You are going to go out. Do you want a post chaise?

SAINT MEGRIN

No.

GEORGES

The weather is stormy.

SAINT MEGRIN

Yes.

(going to the window with a convulsive laugh)

There soon won't be a star in the sky.

GEORGES

And you are going to leave on foot?

SAINT MEGRIN

Yes—on foot.

GEORGES

Unarmed ?

SAINT MEGRIN

I have my sword and dagger. That will suffice—still give me
Schomberg's sword—it is stronger.

(aside)

I am going to see her again—one second and I am at her feet.

GEORGES

Here it is. Do you want me to accompany you?

SAINT MEGRIN

No—I have to go alone.

GEORGES

After midnight—what would your mother say if she knew?

SAINT MEGRIN

My mother—yes—yes—you are right. The storm is growing—my
poor mother—I really want to see her again—if only for an instant.
Listen—you will give her this chain.

(cutting some of his hair with his dagger)

Listen: You will give her these hairs tomorrow if you don't see
me—do you understand?

GEORGES

And why? Why?

SAINT MEGRIN

You don't know, you don't know? Give me my cloak.

GEORGES

My master—my young master—don't leave in the name of heaven—the night will be terrible.

SAINT MEGRIN

Yes, terrible perhaps.

(aside)

Never mind. I have to—she's waiting for me. I've tarried too long. Curses, if I was too late.

GEORGES

In the name of heaven let me follow you.

SAINT MEGRIN

(angrily)

Stay—I order you.

GEORGES

My master!

SAINT MEGRIN

(offering him his hand)

No—embrace me—goodbye—don't forget my mother.

CURTAIN

ACT V

SCENE 6

The room the Duchess is locked in.

The Duchess still has the flowers on her head which she had in the third act—she listens to the clock strike.

DUCHESS

Half past midnight—how slowly the hour drags on. Oh, if he could love me enough not to come. Until one in the morning the doors of the hotel will remain open. I've already seen the Leaguers enter who are meeting here. Doubtless he wasn't with them. Another half hour of anguish and torments—and for the two hours I've been locked in this room, I've only been listening for the noise of his steps. I wanted to pray—to pray—

(listening to someone approaching the door)

Ah, my God! No—no—it's not yet him.

(going to the window)

If this night were less dark, I could see him and by some sign perhaps warn him of the danger, but no hope. The door of the hotel is shut. He's saved for tonight at least. Some obstacle must have kept him from me. Arthur was unable to find him, and perhaps tomorrow, he will in some way learn of the trap into which they hoped to draw him—oh, yes, I'll think of something.

(listening)

I thought I heard—

(going to the door)

Footsteps again—are they those of the Duke? No, no— they're coming up—they're stopping—ah! Coming closer—they're coming.

(with terror)

Don't come in! Don't come in! Flee! Flee—and how? The door was shut behind him. Ah, My God! No hope left!

SAINT MEGRIN

I wasn't mistaken. It was your voice that I heard. It guided me.

DUCHESS

My voice! My voice! It told you to flee.

SAINT MEGRIN

How foolish I was! I couldn't believe in so much happiness.

DUCHESS

That door is still open. Flee, Count, flee!

SAINT MEGRIN

Open, yes—how careless I am!

(he shuts it)

DUCHESS

Count, listen to me.

SAINT MEGRIN

Oh, yes, yes—speak—I need to hear you, to believe my luck.

DUCHESS

Flee! Flee! Death is near—assassins.

SAINT MEGRIN

What are you saying? What's this talk about death and assassins?

DUCHESS

Oh, listen to me—listen to me—in the name of heaven leave this foolish delirium. This goes to life itself, I tell you. They lured you here into an infernal trap. They intend to assassinate you.

SAINT MEGRIN

To assassinate me! This letter wasn't from you?

DUCHESS

It was from me—but through violence, torture. Look—

(showing her bruises)

See!

SAINT MEGRIN

Ha!

DUCHESS

It was I who wrote the letter, but it was the Duke who dictated it.

SAINT MEGRIN

(tearing it)

The Duke—and I believed it? No, no, I didn't believe it for a single instant. My god, my God, my God—she doesn't love me.

DUCHESS

Now, that you know—flee—flee—I told you—he's after your life.

SAINT MEGRIN

She doesn't love me.

(he puts his hand in his chest and beats it)

DUCHESS

Oh, My God! My God!

SAINT MEGRIN

(laughing)

You say it's my life they want. Well, I am going to bring it to them. But without anything to remember you by. Here's this bouquet which my existence has hardly paid for. By one word you're separated me from life like these flowers from their stem. Goodbye, goodbye, forever—

(he tries to reopen the door)

This door is locked.

DUCHESS

It's he. He already knows you are here.

SAINT MEGRIN

Ah, let him come, let him come—Henry, do you have courage only to bruise the arm of a woman? Ah come, come—

DUCHESS

Don't call him! Don't call him. He must come.

SAINT MEGRIN

What do you care? I am indifferent to you—ah, pity—yes.

DUCHESS

But if you will help me, perhaps you could flee.

SAINT MEGRIN

Me flee? And why? My death and my life are events equally foreign to your existence? Flee and would I flee your indifference, your hate perhaps?

DUCHESS

My indifference! My hate—ah—would heaven make it so?

SAINT MEGRIN

Would heaven make it so! You say one word, one word more—and I will obey your blindly—speak—is my death more terrible for you than merely the murder of a man?

DUCHESS

Great God—he asks it—oh, yes, yes—

SAINT MEGRIN

You are not deceiving me! I thank you. You were speaking of fleeing—of ways—what are they? Flee— me—before the Duke of Guise—? Never.

DUCHESS

It's not before the Duke of Guise that you will be fleeing—it's from assassins—Detained in another part of the hotel—by this meeting of Leaguers, he wanted to be certain that once here you wouldn't know how to escape him. If we could only lock this door we would gain a few moments—but the bar's been taken away—a second key is in his hand—and—

(looking)

the other one.

SAINT MEGRIN

Is that it? Wait.

(breaking the point of his dagger in the bolt holder)

Now this door won't open unless it's broken down.

DUCHESS

Good—good—let's find a way—an exit. My ideas are in confusion, my head is splitting.

SAINT MEGRIN

(rushing towards the window)

That window—

DUCHESS

Be very careful—you will kill yourself.

SAINT MEGRIN

Kill myself without vengeance! You are right—I'll wait for them.

DUCHESS

Oh, My God! My God!—Help us—oh, all the measures of vengeance are too well taken—and it's I, I who have not been able to suffer.

(falling to her knees)

Count, in the name of heaven, your pardon.

(rising)

Or rather, no, no don't pardon me—and if you die, I will die with you.

(falling into an armchair)

SAINT MEGRIN

(at her feet)

Well then, make death more sweet. Speak—tell me that you love me—I conjure you with one foot in my grave—I am no more for you than a dying man. The prejudices of the world disappear, the chains of society break before death's agony—Surround my last moments with the joys of heaven. Ah, speak—tell me that I am loved.

DUCHESS

Well, yes, I love you, and for a long while. What struggles I gave myself to flee your eyes, to get away from your voice. Your looks, your words pursued me everywhere—no, for us, society no longer has bonds. The world no longer has prejudices listen to me then, yes, yes, I love you. Here in this very room, from the time I fled a world that your absence depopulated for me—! From the time I came to isolate myself with my love and my tears. And then, I saw you again, your eyes, and I heard your words again and I responded to them. Well—these moments, they've been the sweetest in life.

SAINT MEGRIN

Oh, enough! Enough! You don't want me to be able to face death! Curses! Here—all the happiness of the earth and there death—hell—oh, be quiet—don't tell me anymore that you love me—with your hate I would have braved their daggers—and now, oh, now, I think I'm afraid. Shut up! Shut up!

DUCHESS

Saint Megrin—oh, don't curse me.

SAINT MEGRIN

Yes, yes, I curse you for your love which makes me glimpse heaven and death. To die—young, and be loved by you.

SAINT MEGRIN

Can I die? No, no—tell me again this is only an illusion and a lie!

(noise)

DUCHESS

Listen! Ah—they are here.

SAINT MEGRIN

It's them.

(drawing his sword and leaning on it calmly)

Be off—you've made me weak, foolish—in the face of death I've become a man again. Be off!

DUCHESS

(after a moment's thought)

Saint Megrin—listen—listen—this window, yes I remember there's a balcony on the second floor—if you once reached it—a belt—a cord—you could get down there and then you would escape.

(looking about)

My God—nothing, nothing.

SAINT MEGRIN

Calm yourself, calm, yourself—if I could only make out the balcony—but only over an abyss.

DUCHESS

Listen. You can hear noise in the street.

(rushing to the window)

Whoever you may be—help! Help!

SAINT MEGRIN

(pulling her violently from the window)

What are you doing? Do you want to warn them?

(some cords fall into the room)

What's that?

DUCHESS

Ah, you are saved.

(takes the cord)

Where did it come from? A letter.

(reads)

Some words I overheard have revealed everything to me. I have only this way to save you—and I am employing it—Arthur—Arthur—oh, dear child.

(to Saint Megrin)

It's from Arthur—flee—flee quickly.

SAINT MEGRIN

(attaching the rope)

Well, I have time for it. That door.

(they beat the door violently)

That door.

DUCHESS

Wait—

(She passes her arms between the two iron rings.)

SAINT MEGRIN

Ah, god—what are you doing?

DUCHESS

Leave—leave—it's the arm that was already injured.

SAINT MEGRIN

I prefer to die.

DUKE

(outside—shaking the door)

Open, Madame, open.

DUCHESS

Flee! Flee! By fleeing you will save my life—if you stay I swear I die with you, and I will die dishonored—flee—flee—

SAINT MEGRIN

You will still love me?

DUCHESS

Yes, yes—

DUKE

(outside)

Crowbars and hatchets so I can force this door.

DUCHESS

Leave them—yes—yes—goodbye.

SAINT MEGRIN

Goodbye— Vengeance.

(taking his sword between his teeth, he leaps out the window)

DUCHESS

My god—my god—I thank you—he's saved.

(A moment of silence—the shouts and a clash of arms.)

DUCHESS

Ah!

(She leaves the door and runs to the window.)

DUCHESS

Arthur! Saint Megrin!

(She lets out a second scream and falls in the middle of the stage.)

BLACKOUT

ACT V

SCENE 7

The Duke enters followed by Saint Paul and his henchmen.

DUKE

He got out by the window—but Mayenne will be in the street with twenty men and the roar of arms—Go Saint Paul—follow him— go—and you will tell me if everything is finished.

(knocking against the foot of the Duchess)

Ah, it's you, Madame. Well, I provided you with a tête-à-tête.

DUCHESS

Duke, you had him murdered.

DUKE

Leave me alone, Madame, leave me alone.

DUCHESS

(now hugging his knees)

No, I attach myself to you.

DUKE

Leave me alone, I tell you or rather—yes, yes—come to the light of the torches you can see him one more time.

(He drags her to the window.)

Well—Saint Paul.

SAINT PAUL

(in the street)

Wait—he didn't fall alone—ah! Ah!

DUKE

Is it he?

SAINT PAUL

No—it's the little page.

DUCHESS

Arthur—ah, poor child.

DUKE

They've let him get away—the wretches.

DUCHESS

(hopefully)

Oh—

SAINT PAUL

Here he is.

DUKE

Dead?

SAINT PAUL

No—covered with wounds but breathing still.

DUCHESS

He's breathing. They can save him. Duke in the name of heaven.

SAINT PAUL

He must have some talisman against iron and fire.

DUKE

(tearing the Duchess' handkerchief off)

Well, here—strangle him with this handkerchief— death will be sweeter for him—it has the arms of the Duchess on it.

DUCHESS

Ah.

(she falls)

DUKE

(after having looked in the street for a moment)

Good and now that were done with the valet, let's occupy ourselves with his master, the king.

CURTAIN

ABOUT THE TRANSLATOR

Frank J. Morlock has written and translated many plays since retiring from the legal profession in 1992. His translations have also appeared on Project Gutenberg, the Alexandre Dumas Père web page, Literature in the Age of Napoléon, InfiniteArtistries. com, and Munsey's (formerly Blackmask). In 2006 he received an award from the North American Jules Verne Society for his translations of Verne's plays. He lives and works in México.